MW01108403

Sipping in the City:
Beyond your grandmother's tea room

New York – the ideal city for theater-goers, art lovers, and...tea sippers? It's true. The metropolis that provides a backdrop for great plays and inspiring paintings also is home to an unequaled array of tea venues. From the grandeur of the Astor Court at the St. Regis to the casual fun of Alice's Tea Cup, taking tea in New York is marked by charm and variety. *Tea in the City: New York* is an indispensable guide to tea rooms and tea shops great and small in North America's largest city.

Elizabeth Knight is uniquely suited to be your guide to tea in New York. She has intimately known and loved the city for more than 22 years, and currently serves as the Tea Sommelier at the city's historic St. Regis Hotel. She is author of such popular books as *Tea With Friends* and *Welcome Home*. Elizabeth also has written numerous articles on tea, entertaining, and travel for *Romantic Homes* magazine and various tea publications.

Tea in City: New York is the first in our new series of guidebooks that will help you experience the world's great cities with tea on your mind.

Bruce Richardson
Benjamin Press

Other books in this series:
Tea in the City: London
Tea in the City: Paris

Tea in the City:
New York

A tea lover's guide
to sipping and shopping
in the city

Elizabeth Knight
Photographs by Bruce Richardson

TEA ROOMS TEA SHOPS TEA BARS TEA WARES
HOTEL TEAS CAFE TEAS MUSEUM TEAS

BENJAMIN PRESS
PO Box 100
Perryville, Kentucky 40468
800.765.2139
www.benjaminpress.com

ISBN 0-9663478-7-0
Printed in China through Four Colour Imports, Ltd.

Every effort has been made to guarantee the accu-
racy of listings in this guidebook. But in a city that
never sleeps, change is constant. Avoid disap-
pointment by phoning to verify information before
setting out on the tea trail.

Tea in the City:
An invitation

My mother taught me to love tea and New York. She'd grown up right across the river in New Jersey, and considered the city her backyard. I was in the sixth grade the year we moved from El Paso, Texas, to Taranto, Italy, with a stopover in New York. We bought pretzels from a pushcart, attended mass at St. Patrick's, and took in a Broadway musical. Standing next to my mother on top of the Empire State building, I looked uptown toward Central Park and whispered, "I'm going to live here someday. "

It took longer than planned, but eventually I did live in a fifth-floor walk-up in a "neighborhood in transition." Translation – it was so scary that no one would visit after dark. I've never felt more at home anywhere. As an Air Force brat, I had encountered places where I didn't feel welcome, but in New York, I was just another immigrant, along with all the other hopefuls from one hundred seventy-three countries.

New York is both the quintessential American city and another country. Here, just by hopping a subway, it is possible to visit a dozen foreign countries in an afternoon and take home their food, clothing, and art.

I never tire of it, but when I'm exhausted from a day trying to bite all of the Big Apple, I enjoy a relaxing cup of tea. Please use this guide to discover the perfect place in New York to share an experience with a friend you don't yet know.

Elizabeth Knight

Elizabeth Knight

Tea in the City: New York
A tea lover's guide
to sipping and shopping in the city

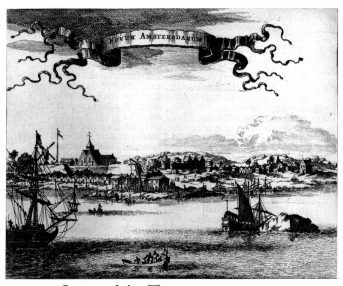

Steeped in Tea:
New York before the Manhattan

Manhattan might have a cocktail named after it, but did you know that the city's first fashionable beverage was tea? Americans drank tea before the British, and New Yorkers drank it first.

Dutch mariners introduced the "excellent China drink" to Amsterdam in 1606, and some historians say that peg-legged Peter Stuyvesant brought tea with him in 1647 when he was appointed governor of Manhattan. Seventeenth-century sippers enjoyed both Japanese green and Chinese black teas. *Orange-Pekoe*, named for the Dutch Royal House of Orange, remains well known.

Dutch *thee* became English *tee* or tea when New Amsterdam was forced to surrender to the British in 1664. The colony was re-christened New York to honor James, Duke of York, brother of King Charles II. Queens, New York's largest borough, was named for Catherine of Braganza, Charles' Portuguese bride, who was England's first tea-drinking queen.

Wealthy New Yorkers – Dutch and British – drank tea twice a day. Tea parties with Dutch *koeckjes* (cookies) were a popular form of entertainment. New York's most famous tea party occurred on April 22, 1774, when rebellious colonials tossed eighteen chests of that "pernicious British herb" into New York harbor to protest the tax on tea.

Although tea drinking was considered unpatriotic during the Revolutionary War years, General George Washington must have enjoyed it while

George Washington, inaugurated at the old City Hall, was said to breakfast daily on three cups of tea.

headquartered at the Morris-Jumel mansion during the Battle of Harlem Heights. His household inventory recorded several sets of Chinese and Wedgwood tewares. When a stash of tea was discovered hidden in some woods, Washington personally wrote orders for its distribution to his Colonial Army officers.

New York City became the capital of the new nation in 1784. Washington, inaugurated at the old City Hall, was said to breakfast daily on three cups of tea. Tea water pumps, erected over freshwater springs, provided the President and citizens with potable water for a penny or two a pail.

Eighteenth-century New York boasted two hundred tea establishments. Gardens, named Ranelagh and Vauxhall after their London counterparts,

Washington Irving described a tea table in The Legend of Sleepy Hollow: *"Such heaped-up platters of cake of various and almost indescribable kinds, known only to experienced Dutch housewives ... all mingled higgledy-piggledy, with the mother tea-pot sending up its clouds of vapor from the midst."*

sprang up around the Lower East Side and the Bowery. Here, city sophisticates could stroll through leafy glades, flirt, or sit to sip tea.

Ships sped between New York Harbor and Asia clipping the time it took to satisfy America's thirst for tea, porcelain, and silk. In 1808, John Jacob Astor's ship, *The Beaver*, sailed for Canton loaded with $45,000 worth of fur and other goods. She returned with $200,000 worth of Chinese tea, helping the once-penniless German immigrant become America's first multimillionaire.

The Great Atlantic and Pacific Tea Company opened on Vesey Street in 1859 and grew into the world's largest chain store, the ancestor of today's A&P grocery. By 1860, $8.3 million worth of imported tea was handled by New York merchants.

Today, the tradition of afternoon
tea continues to gather steam.
Locals like to celebrate
a birthday, bridal shower,
or other special event
with a convivial tea party.

Today, the tradition of afternoon tea continues to gather steam. Locals like to celebrate a birthday, bridal shower, or other special event with a convivial tea party. Jet-lagged travelers find afternoon tea a soothing late lunch or early dinner. Tea makes a light yet satisfying pre-theatre or post-concert meal. Afternoon teas are edging out cocktail parties as busy executives discover they can conduct business with cups that cheer but don't inebriate. Parched shoppers and footsore tourists revive drooping spirits with time-out over tea.

Although an English-style afternoon tea is among the oldest of New York's tea traditions, it is only one way to enjoy a fragrant cup. Today, in the East Village neighborhood once home to Peter Stuyvesant's farm, it is possible to sip Japanese matcha, Moroccan mint, Tibetan bocha, and Taiwanese bubble tea. Leave your passport at home; New York is the world in a tea cup!

New York City: Orientation 101

Navigating the streets of New York can be daunting, even for natives of the city. To help you find that one special tea room - or a cluster of tea shops in a particular district - *Tea in the City* features a color-coded map. Each section of the guidebook highlights one section of the city, making it easy to identify tea rooms that may be within a few blocks of each other. A comprehensive index at the back of the guidebook can direct you to an individual tea room.

- Lower Manhattan
- Chinatown and the Lower East Side
- SoHo and NoLita
- Greenwich Village
- West Village
- East Village
- Chelsea and the Meat-Packing District
- Gramercy Park, Kips Bay and Union Square
- Midtown East
- Midtown West
- Upper East Side
- Upper West Side
- Harlem and Upper Manhattan
- The Boroughs: Brooklyn, The Bronx, Queens, Staten Island

Eighty-nine of the tea rooms cited in Tea in the City *are located in Manhattan, with an additional twelve located in the boroughs of the Bronx, Queens, and Brooklyn. Please note that the guide map is not drawn to scale, and all designated boundaries are approximate.*

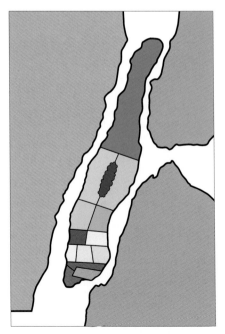

Lower Manhattan

New York was born over four hundred years ago on the southern tip of Manhattan overlooking the natural harbor now home to the Statue of Liberty and Ellis Island. The area includes neighborhoods such as **Battery Park** (named for the battery of cannon that defended the young city), **TriBeCa** (the triangle below Canal Street), and **Wall Street** (named for a wooden palisade that protected the original Dutch settlement). Lower Manhattan was badly damaged by the terrorist attacks in 2001, but Ground Zero has been cleaned up and downtown is back in business.

Lobby Lounge at the Ritz-Carlton Hotel, Battery Park
Two West Street at Battery Place

The Art Deco-inspired Lobby Lounge hosts an afternoon tea as well as high tea. Afternoon tea, served on Wedgwood's *Persia* pattern, includes sophisticated tea sandwiches that change seasonally – trout with mustard, *carpaccio* (beef) and tomato, fresh *rabiola* (goat's milk) cheese with Muscat grapes and smoked chicken, an Asian cracker with seared tuna and sesame-seaweed salad with quail egg, cucumber, caviar and smoked salmon on pumpernickel with crème fraiche, and *prosciutto* (ham)-wrapped asparagus. Assorted tea breads, warm raisin scones with Devonshire cream, lemon curd and raspberry *coulis,* and decadent mini pastries including a berry-fruit tart, chocolate Opera cake, madeleines, and macaroons, as well as pistachio and vanilla *pots de crème*, will satisfy the most discriminating sweet tooth. Taylors of Harrogate supplies eleven types of loose tea, including their famous Yorkshire Gold blend.

For those with bolder tastes, the Ritz-Carlton offers a Power High Tea beginning with a bracing tea cocktail infused with mint, berry or apple vodka. Savories, served in successive courses, include a mini brioche sandwich with smoked trout, a crock of seared foie gras spread, toasted walnut country bread, steak tartare with *gaufrette* potatoes (gourmet chips) and a mini Stilton cheese souffle.

• Closed Sundays. Open Mon.-Sat. 2-5pm • Subway: 1 train to Rector St., 4/5 trains to Bowling Green • Tel. 212-344-0800 • Reservations recommended • Dress code: business casual • Major credit cards • www.ritzcarlton.com • Full set afternoon and high tea. $$$

The Ritz Carlton's Rise Bar with its outdoor terrace is famous for the 180-degree harbor view. The Battery Park esplanade is within walking distance, along with the Irish Hunger Memorial, Museum of Jewish Heritage, Skyscraper Museum, National Museum of the American Indian, Wall Street, and the World Trade Center site.

Yaffa's Tea Room
353 Greenwich St. or 19 Harrison St.

"Don't think – just do!" is Yaffa's motto. First, she opened a bistro-bar on the corner of Greenwich Street, then a tea room in an adjacent space on Harrison Street. The artist scoured flea markets and raided dumpsters for bits and bobs which she re-wired and re-painted to transform the interior into a bohemian Mediterranean tea room.

Tea here is funky, not fancy, and service can be quirky at best. But the neighborhood loves Yaffa because she kept the place open 24/7 in the chaotic months following the attacks on nearby Ground Zero. "People started coming in to feel secure," she says. Sleeping quarters were set up in the tea room for rescue workers, and the restaurant prepared food for people suddenly living without water, phones, or electricity.

TriBeCa (the triangle below Canal Street) is located south of Canal Street, north of Chambers Street, and west of Broadway. Artists seeking inexpensive studio space fled SoHo for this area with a Hudson River view. Galleries, chic boutiques, antique stores, and a funky tea room are part of the neighborhood's raffish charm.

The High Tea menu draws on Yaffa's eclectic background. Born in Tunisia to a well-to-do family, she once lived in a Bedouin tent and drank rosebud tea with honey and milk. Twenty teas, including Earl Grey and green, but mostly herbals, are on offer. *Petits choux* stuffed with *duxelle* (finely-chopped mushrooms, shallots and herbs) or egg salad, *petite croque monsieur* (grilled ham and cheese) and *croque madame* (chicken and cheese), and croutons with gravlax and dill sauce, are interesting alternatives to standard tea sandwiches. Scones with jelly and a variety of home-baked desserts - pear tarte Tatin, tiramisu, chocolate truffle cake, and crème brulee - complete her interpretation.

• Afternoon tea served daily 2-6pm • Subway: 1 train to Franklin St. • Tel. 212-274-9403 • Reservations required at least 24 hours in advance • Major credit cards • Tea by the pot. Set tea. Snacks. Sweets. $$

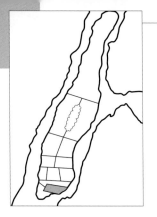

Chinatown and the Lower East Side

Chinese immigrants founded **Chinatown**, the largest in the United States, in the late 1870s. Sights and sounds here make it easy to imagine that you are in the nation where tea drinking began. After experiencing this area's many tea houses, you'll know that *Precious Eyebrow* is a delectable tea and *Dim Sum* is a mouth-watering brunch. (For some useful terms and a quick look at China's tea history, see page 18.) New York's adjacent southeastern corner – now known as the **Lower East Side** – was home to freed African-American slaves, who were followed by waves of Irish, Jewish, German, and Italian immigrants who lived in tumbledown tenements and hawked goods from pushcarts. Today the historic streets and landmark buildings are being reborn with boutiques, spas, and restaurants, along with a Chinese tea gallery and a tea room owned by a rock musician.

Dim Sum GoGo
5 E. Broadway btwn. Catherine St. and Chatham Sq.

Unlike many traditional tea houses, this one prepares dim sum from morning to night. Twenty-four types of dumplings are offered in this restaurant with a cheery red and white décor.
• Daily 10am-11pm • Subway: F train to East Broadway, 4/5/6 trains to Chamber St. or City Hall • Tel. 212-732-0797 • Major credit cards • Tea by the pot. Entrees. Dim Sum. $

Dragon Land Bakery
125 Walker St. near Baxter & Canal Sts.

A modern bakery café with a wide assortment of sweet and savory buns, cakes, and tapioca bubble tea drinks. Sit and watch the hectic street scene or get a snack to-go.
• Daily 7:30am-8pm • Subway: J/N/R/Q/W/Z/6 trains to Canal St. • Tel. 212-219-2012 • Cash only • Cup of tea. Bubble tea. Snacks. $

Green Tea Cafe
45 Mott St. btwn. Bayard and Pell Sts.

Green Tea café opened in 2000 determined to bring excitement to an ancient beverage. The menu is as modern as the music bouncing off the exposed brick walls. The café offers a dozen bubble teas and another dozen flavored milk-teas (strawberry, honeydew, peanut, coconut, taro). Sixteen fruit and floral green teas, ten flavored black teas, including one mixing tea, coffee, milk and honey, are offered. There's also Thai iced tea with tapioca and a variety of fruit smoothies. Green Tea Cafe offers a selection of sweets, sandwiches, snacks, and exotic specialties including matcha yogurt with matcha jelly, or thick toast in a puddle of coconut milk.

• Daily 10:30am-midnight; weekends til 2am • Subway: J/N/R/Q/W/Z/6 trains to Canal St. • www.greenteacafe.com • Tel. 212-693-2888 • Cash only • Pot of tea. Bubble tea. Sandwiches. Snacks. $

Mandarin Court
61 Mott Street, btwn. Bayard and Canal Sts.

It's always a good sign when a place is full of Chinese families. Mandarin Court is not big on atmosphere, but it has lots of delicious food, served from rolling steam carts, by efficient waiters.
• Daily 8am-11pm • Subway: J/N/R/Q/W/Z/6 trains to Canal St. • Tel. 212-608-3838 • Major credit cards • Tea by the pot. Dim Sum. Entrees. $

May-May Gourmet Dim Sum and Bakery
35 Pell St. btwn. Bowery and Mott Sts.

Should you yen to host a dim sum tea party in your own home, stop by May-May ("double happiness"). The shop, which has supplied restaurant chefs for forty years, sells countless varieties of delicious dumplings, buns, sweet and savory pastries, and tamales.
• Daily 8am-7pm • Subway: J/N/R/Q/W/Z/ 6 trains to Canal St. • Tel. 212-267-0733 • www.maymayfood.com • Major credit cards

Green tea ice cream.

Nom Wah Tea Parlor
13 Doyers St. at Pell St.

Some say that the 90-degree turn onto Doyers Street was engineered to stop evil ghosts. Chinatown's oldest tea house (1920), which was recently featured in a Spiderman movie, offers more than 20 varieties of tea including jasmine, green, and oolong served in simple metal pots.
• Daily 10:30am-7pm • Subway: J/N/R/Q/ W/Z/6 trains to Canal St. • Tel. 212-962-6047 • Cash only • Tea by the pot. Snacks. $

Silk Road Place
30 Mott St. btwn. Bayard and Chatham Sq.

An East-meets-West café and tourist information center where you can check e-mail, sip bubble tea, and nosh Krispy Kreme doughnuts or Chinese snacks. Downstairs, on Friday nights, (8-10 pm), *Teabag Open Mic* presents live entertainment. Free admission. *Teabag: Amplified* is a musician's showcase held the first Saturday of each month. Shows start at 8pm; admission is $10.
• Daily 9am-10pm • Subway: J/N/R/Q/W/ Z/6 trains to Canal St. • Tel. 212-566-3738 • Cash only • Bubble tea. Snacks. $

Sweet-n-Tart Restaurant
20 Mott St. btwn. Worth & Mosco Sts.

Skip the basement level and head directly to the third floor where service and atmosphere are more pleasant. Four different menus are available. In addition to dim sum cooked to order, there are dishes prepared according to ancient principles of Chinese medicine, traditional entrees, and an extensive list of tea beverages including hot and cold Taiwan-style and sago drinks - taro, coconut, and almond milk tea. Red (black to non-Chinese) tea selections include tea with honey, sago or lemon. Green tea comes with cinnamon, sago, honey or mint. There are fourteen kinds of fruit shakes made with milk or tapioca pearls, sugar cane juice and other specialty drinks. Bubble tea offered. (Original café at 76 Mott St. has a more limited menu.)

• Daily 10am-midnight • Subway: J/N/R/Q/ W/Z/6 trains to Canal St. • Tel. 212-964-0380 • Credit card minimum $25 • Pot of tea. Dim Sum. Entrees. $

Sun Hop Shing Tea House
21 Mott St. btwn. Worth & Mosco Sts.

If the hustle of the larger houses is too much, head for this small, no-frills restaurant. Fragrant jasmine tea, brewed with loose leaves, is served in a large metal pot; no charge with a food order.

• Daily 7:30am-7pm • Subway: J/N/R/Q/ W/Z/6 trains to Canal St. • Tel. 212-267-2729 • Cash only • Tea by pot. Dim sum. Entrees. $

Tai Pan Bakery
194 Canal St.

A wide assortment of freshly baked cakes, sweet breads, four types of egg custard tarts, hot snacks, and sweet or savory buns are available at this and the Queens location.
• Daily 7:30am-8pm • Subway: J/N/R/Q/ W/Z/6 trains to Canal St. • Tel. 212-732-2222 • Cash only • www.taipan-bakery.com • Tea by cup. Bubble tea. Snacks. Sweets. $

Tea & Tea
51 Mott St., btwn. Bayard and Pell Sts.

Two 20-year-old Chinese immigrants opened Tea & Tea, in 1999, when they realized bubble tea was hot. Today, their casually furnished cafe is packed with young Asians and Americans. Customers may select from fifteen "exotic" drinks such as *Verdant Cooler,* a refreshing blend of green tea, peppermint, passion fruit juice and honey. There's jasmine, blueberry, lemon and several other green tea blends, nine flavored black teas, and eleven frothy tapioca teas. Fruity milk shakes, smoothies and an extensive "nutritious natural series," such as red grapefruit with aloe vera, provide a beverage for

every taste. Ask for a frequent sipper's card; the tenth regular-sized drink is complimentary. American-style snacks are balanced by Chinese "authentic delicacies" such as vegetable spring rolls, rabbit-shaped buns, chicken wings, and jumbo tea eggs. Green tea cheesecake is a new twist on a New York standard.

• Sun.-Fri. 11am-11:30pm, Sat. 11am-midnight • Subway: J/N/R/Q/W/Z/6 trains to Canal St. • Tel. 212-766-9889 • Cash only
• Pot of tea. Bubble tea. Snacks. Sweets. $

Ten Ren Tea & Ginseng Co., Inc.
75 Mott St., btwn. Bayard & Canal Sts.

Founded in 1953, the Ten Ren ("heavenly love") company is one of the largest tea growers and manufacturers in East Asia. Tea lovers head here for fine Chinese and Taiwanese teas. Hostesses greet shoppers with sample-sized cups of the freshly brewed tea of the day. There is also an attractively decorated tasting alcove where customers may sit, sip, and savor.

Dozens of loose tea varieties, some costing more than $100 per pound, are stored in large gold-colored metal canisters. In addition to standards (Pu-erh, Pouchong, and Ti-Kuan Yin), the shop carries fine oolongs, including a green Tung Ting. Decaffeinated orange-spice, plum, and ginger tea lift the spirits without keeping you up at night. Decorative red or floral brocade gift boxes present two or more beautifully packaged containers of premium teas.

Bubble tea originated in Taiwan in the 1980's as a treat for children. Marble-sized pearls made of sweetened starch from the cassava plant or sago palm are added to green or black tea with fruit, or fruit juice, and milk. The hot or cold mix is shaken vigorously to produce bubbles and served with a fat straw to suck the chewy pearls.

All the utensils necessary for brewing and serving tea properly are sold here: Western-style teapots, timers, tea sacs and strainers, electric kettles, and decorative, silvery air-tight storage tins. A wide assortment of Chinese-style ceramic funnels, tea boats, tea containers, trays, towels, waste-water bowls, and dregs spoons are available. Pots and cups in a breathtaking variety of colors, styles, and shapes, including animals of the Chinese zodiac, are beautifully displayed. Owners John and Ellen Lii also teach classes on the art of making Chinese-style tea.

• Daily 10am-8pm • Subway: J/N/R/Q/W/Z/6 trains to Canal St. • Tel. 212-349-2286
• www.tenrenusa.com • Major credit cards

Ten Ren's Tea Time
79 Mott St., btwn. Bayard & Canal Sts.

Ten Ren's first bubble tea bar is located just a few doors from the company store. Designed to attract young people, bouncy Taiwanese pop tunes blare as patrons place orders at the sleek white counter. In addition to two dozen hot or iced tapioca teas, including Oriental Beauty, Tung-Ting Oolong, and Hibiscus teas, customers may order green tea or fruit-flavored shakes. Tapioca Shredded Ice is available blended with mango, peach, passion fruit, taro, red bean, green bean, and green tea, among eight other flavors. Fifteen types of fruit, nut, and bean Taiwanese Slush Ices, with a variety of toppings, make for a sweet treat.

Tea Time offers a dozen varieties of "traditional" premium green teas and seven black hot teas including their own King's Tea 319 and a fragrant lavender-black blend. You can eat your tea, too. Sticky rice, noodles, tea eggs, tea jellies, cheesecake and scones, all made with green tea, are offered.

• Sun.-Thu. 11am-11pm; Fri.-Sat.11am-midnight • Subway: J/N/R/Q/W/Z/6 trains to Canal St. • Tel. 212-732-7178 • Cash only • www.tenren.usa.com • Cup of tea. Bubble tea. Snacks. Sweets. $

Ten Ren
138 Lafayette St. btwn. Canal & Howard Sts. (Holiday Inn bldg.)
• Daily 10am-8pm • Subway: J/N/R/Q/W/Z/6 trains to Canal St. • Tel. 212-343-8090
• Cup of tea. Bubble tea. Retail. $

Chinese Tea Traditions

Legend holds that Emperor Shen Nung, the Divine Healer, drank boiled water for his health. One day, about 5,000 years ago, leaves from a *Camellia sinensis* bush blew into a container of water that servants were boiling in his garden. The emperor sampled, pronounced it delightful, and ordered all his subjects to drink the new brew. Tea houses developed as early as the Tang Dynasty (618-907 AD). Chinese people still gather at them, even in New York, to socialize, conduct business, and settle disputes.

Dim sum ("touch the heart"), traditionally served 8am-2pm, includes sweet and savory tidbits such as meat, vegetable or seafood dumplings, rice porridge, thousand-year-old eggs, cakes, buns, and tarts taken with tea. Hong Kong-style dim sum is served by waitresses pushing metal carts with built-in heaters. They stop at each table to announce the contents, usually in sing-song Cantonese, sometimes in English, or simply lift the lids on steamers stacked in their carts, to display contents. Ask for something specific or just point to whatever looks good.

Most tea houses don't take reservations unless the party numbers fifteen or more. If your group is smaller than four, offer to share a table. Dim sum tea rooms are likely to be

---

Teas Typically Served with Dim Sum

- *Bo Lei* (Puerh in Mandarin) – Dark, earthy-tasting tea thought to aid digestion and lower cholesterol. To order, tug on your earlobe.
- *Dragon Well* (Longjing or Lung Ching) – Light, slightly sweet green tea grown in Zhejiang province. Believed to cool you down in hot weather.
- *Precious Eyebrow* (Chun Mei, Chunmee, Sowmee, Show Mee, Zhen Mei) - Eyebrow-shaped green leaves that brew a mellow, plum-flavored tea. To order, trace your eyebrow from nose to ear, with your index finger.
- *Guk Fa* or *Kwok Fah* (Chrysanthemum) – Infusion of dried chrysanthemum flowers usually served with rock sugar in the pot or on the side.
- *Guk Bo* – Combination of Bo Lei and Guk Fa.
- *Oolong* – A delicate fruity, flowery tea grown in Fujian province and Taiwan.
- *Sui Sin* or *Soy Sin* (Water Fairy) – Believed to help cure colds. To order, simulate a wave with your arm.
- *Ti Kuan Yin* or *Teet Kwun Yum* (Iron Goddess of Mercy or Iron Buddha) – Slightly sweet, honey-colored oolong tea with a delicate floral aroma. Said to help lower cholesterol.

noisy and crowded, but that's part of the fun. Don't be put off by the lack of décor; the focus is on the food.

At some restaurants, patrons order from a slip of paper with a number assigned to each item. In others, servers stamp a card to record each dish ordered. It is customary to order a variety of textures and flavors to share with companions.

Usually, there's a per person charge for tea. Tea is placed on the table to help guests refresh themselves and to aid digestion. It is not served with food unless requested. Non-Chinese are usually given a jasmine or oolong tea, but consult the sidebar for other suggestions. Don't worry if you can't pronounce them; some teas may be ordered with sign language!

If you order multiple types of tea, they're likely to be served all-at-once and you won't be told which is which. Tea will be brewed with loose leaves, left in the pot. Flip a metal pot's lid up, or slot a ceramic lid diagonally into the pot's mouth, to signal that you want more tea or hot water. Custom dictates that the person seated closest to the teapot pours for the entire table. Polite people always serve themselves last. Cantonese rap knuckles or tap the table twice, with index or middle finger, to indicate thanks.

The Tea Gallery
131 Allen St. at Delancey St. (Lower East Side)

Michael and Winnie Wong, owners of Wong & Sons Art Gallery, met when she was studying architecture and he was searching for antiques for his family's art gallery. When Michael decided to serve customers tea, both studied with famed Hong Kong tea masters. Today, the gallery sells exquisite ceramics, furniture, and art as well as a wide range of high quality Chinese teas: white, green, black, red, exotic oolongs, aged Puerhs, jasmine, and other scented teas. The Wongs specialize in seasonal teas such as Dragon Well from Lion Peak or West Lake, and Mt. East Biluochun. Enthusiasts drop in for a fine cup of tea brewed with water boiled with Mongolian wheat-rice rocks. Michael feels that the rocks improve the texture of the water resulting in a smoother, sweeter tea. Call ahead if you'd like to arrange a private tea-tasting session.

• Tues.-Sat. 11am-7pm; Sun. 1:30pm-6pm
• Subway: F/J/M/Z trains to Delancey/Essex Sts. • Tel. 217-777-6148

TeaNY
90 Rivington St. btwn. Ludlow & Orchard Sts. (Lower East Side)

Richard Melville Hall, the great-great-grand nephew of Herman Melville, author of *Moby Dick*, was born in Harlem but lives and works downtown. Moby, as the techno-rock musician is now known, opened a hip tea room in 2000 with partner Kelly Tisdale. TeaNY rocks nearly round the clock even though

The Lower East Side Tenement Museum, 90 Orchard St. at Broome St., gives a glimpse of immigrant life.
• Tel. 212-431-0233
• Reservations recommended
• www.tenement.org

neither of them had any previous restaurant experience. Presentation and service can be spotty, but artists and other young fans rave about the prices, the vegan and vegetarian menus, and the tea list – over ninety choices. For a modest price, you're served two scones with butter and jam, two types of tea sandwiches from a choice of five, a brownie, two biscotti or other mini-dessert, and a pot of tea. Loose tea, bottled iced tea and juice drinks, teapots, mugs, and other "teany stuff" are for sale along with *The Teany Book: Stories, Food, Romance, Cartoons and, Of Course, Tea.*

• Fri.-Sat. 10am-2am, Sun. 10am-8pm. Closed Thanksgiving and Christmas • Subway: F/J/M/Z trains to Delancey St., V train to 2nd Ave. • Tel. 212-475-9190 • Major credit cards • www.teany.com • Tea by the pot. Cream tea. A la carte vegan and vegetarian selections. $

Shopping Sites for Tea Lovers

Jade Garden Arts and Crafts Co.
76 Mulberry St. btwn. Bayard and Canal Sts.

Reasonably priced Yixing teapots in a range of colors and shapes. Ceramic flowerpots and figurines. • Daily 10am-7pm • Subway: B/D trains to Grand St. • Tel. 212-587-5685

Kam Man Supermarket
200 Canal St. at Mulberry St.

The original – and possibly the best – all-in-one Asian emporium in New York. The first floor is crowded with spices, sauces, and delicacies such as dried shark fins. Downstairs, tea fans will find three walls of colorfully packaged teas, including white, green, black, oolong, lychee, lotus, mango, mint, passion fruit, ginseng root, ginger-honey, barley, Long-Life, Beauty-Slim, and De-Tox.

Thirty-six large, clear jars display loose tea including Pio Lo Chun, Precious Eyebrow, Ginseng oolong-green, Young Hyson, Yunnan, and White Peony. There are several types of puerh including Tuocha, which looks like a baby bird's nest. Small containers hold dried rosebuds, nasturtium, magnolia, honeysuckle, and jasmine flowers for making your own blends. Bubble tea fans will find tapioca pearls and inexpensive packs of brightly-colored, wide-mouthed straws. Ceramic dinnerware, including tea sets with pots and cups, sell for as little as $10. Tea brewing accessories include Eastern-style bamboo baskets and Western-style steel mesh strainers and infuser balls.
• Daily 8:30am-8:45pm • Subway: A/C/E/N/R/J/M/Z/6 trains to Canal St. • Tel. 212-571-0330 • www.kammanfood.com

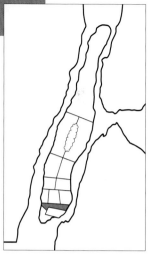

SoHo and NoLita

Houston Street is the dividing line for several neighborhoods in the southern end of New York, producing the nicknames **SoHo** (<u>so</u>uth of <u>Ho</u>uston Street) and **NoHo** (<u>no</u>rth of <u>Ho</u>uston Street). **NoLita** stands for <u>no</u>rth of <u>Li</u>ttle <u>I</u>taly. In the 1960s artists began turning 19th-century cast iron industrial buildings into lofts and galleries. Developers swooped in, the artists moved out, and now the beautifully restored structures house trendy boutiques and branches of suburban mall stores.

Athélier Tea Workshop (Tea Bar at DKNY)
420 W. Broadway (enter from Thompson St. btwn. Prince & Spring Sts.)

Growing up in Paraguay, Xavier de Leon learned from rain forest natives the benefits of hundreds of herbs and flowers. In Paris the long-time tea lover studied to become a certified tea connoisseur. In 2000 he co-founded Societhé New York to position tea as a fashionable, healthy, and profitable alternative to coffee. His New York-based business, Athélier Tea Workshop, includes an emporium, catering services, and the boutique-style Tea Bar at Donna Karan's Soho store, which opened in 2004.

Yerba maté, a high-caffeine beverage made from the bark of a South American tree, is a popular offering at Athélier.

The Tea Bar is a contemporary, cosmopolitan fusion of East-West with brick walls, vintage tea posters, and metal stools. Over 80 of the owner's handpicked, custom-blended teas are on the menu along with fruit-flavored iced tea and hundreds of herbal infusions. *Thequino,* made with yerba mate and foamed milk, is Xavier's delicious take on the traditional Paraguayan nutritional pick-me-up drink. Tea is also an ingredient in a number of sweet and savory dishes – a smoked turkey sandwich with Lapsang Souchong tea mayonnaise, a salad with Sencha Caesar dressing and matcha croutons, and Early Grey chocolate cake. Athélier sells bulk loose tea and creates custom blends.
• Daily 11am-7pm • Subway: N/R/W trains to Prince St, C/E trains to Spring St. • www.atheliertea.com • Tel. 646-613-8996 • Tea by the pot. Snacks. Sweets. $

Cendrillon Asian Grill and Merienda Bar
45 Mercer St. btwn. Broome & Grand Sts.

In many countries with Hispanic heritage, the meal served between lunch and dinner is called *merienda. Merienda* may be an afternoon tea, a child's after-school snack, or a refreshing break in the work day. Philippine-born Romy Dorotan has drawn on traditions

of his home country, along with those of Spain, China, and Malaysia, to create innovative dishes. Praised in *The New York Times*, *The Wall Street Journal*, and *Gourmet* magazine, the restaurant is a long narrow room softened by a glass skylight. Thick wooden tables, brick walls hung with Filipino arts and crafts, and glowing votive candles warm the loft-like space.

Although the traditional beverages served in Filipino tea houses are rice-coffee, hot chocolate, lime or coconut juice, you may order a pot of freshly brewed loose tea. Thirteen standards plus herbals are available. Try the Dragon-Eyes, a Chinese black tea blended with a small fruit similar to lychee.

Begin with an order of *Ukoy* – shrimp, bean sprout, and tofu fritters, followed by classic merienda dishes – *Pancit Luglug*, thick rice noodles with shrimp, smoked trout, pork and tofu; *Bibingka*, a delicious rice and coconut milk pancake, baked in banana leaves, topped with feta and Gouda cheese; or *Turon*, fried plantain and jackfruit wrapped in edible rice paper, deep fried, then sprinkled with sugar. Save room for *Halo-Halo* ("mix-mix"), an exotic iced dessert composed of layered red beans, coconut, jackfruit, sugar-palm, coconut-pineapple gel, and toasted green rice, topped with flan and purple yam ice cream. It makes plain old vanilla seem too tame.

• Closed Mondays. Open Sun. and Tues.-Thurs. 11am-10pm; Fri. and Sat. til 10:30pm. Merienda dishes served Sat.-Sun. • Subway: R/W trains to Prince St., 6 train to Spring St. • Tel. 212-343-9012 • Reservations recommended • Major credit cards • www.cendrillon.com • Pot of tea. Entrees. Snacks. Sweets. $$

The Housing Works Used Book Shop
126 Crosby St. south of Houston St.

Housing Works is a not-for-profit organization that provides housing, services, and advocacy for homeless people living with HIV and AIDS. The two-story used book store contains over 45,000 books and records arranged by category. The shop hosts author readings and live music performances. The volunteer-run café sells freshly prepared snacks, sweets, and cups of bagged tea.
• Mon.-Fri. 10 am-9pm, Sat. noon-9pm, Sun. noon-7pm • Subway: N/R/W trains to Prince St.; F/V trains to Broadway/Lafayette St.; 6 train to Spring St. • Tel. 212-334-3324 • www.housingworksubc.com • Cup of tea. Snacks. Sweets. $

Kelley and Ping
127 Greene St. btwn. Prince & Houston Sts.

Kelley and Ping is a combination tea shop, Asian grocery, and noodle bar. The Soho location's open kitchen is set up to suggest market stalls in China, Vietnam, Korea, and Thailand, with food cooked before your eyes. Over two dozen freshly brewed teas are served in big metal pots accompanied by thick, handle-less cups. On a sultry day, sit on a stool under the ceiling fan with a tall Thai iced tea in one hand and a large walnut cookie in the other. The wall behind the cash register is stocked with glass canisters and decorative tins containing fourteen types of loose tea for sale including Chrysanthemum, Genmaicha, Gunpowder and Iron Goddess of Mercy, lotus, lemon, spice, and vanilla. (Second location Gramercy Park.)
• Daily 11:30am-11pm • Subway: N/R trains to Prince St., F train to Broadway-Lafayette • Tel. 212-228-1212 • Major credit cards • www.kelleyandping.com • Tea by the pot. Snacks. $

Gunpowder tea (a hand-rolled green tea from China) got its name from the tiny pellet-shaped leaves that, to Western eyes, resembled gunpowder.

Lahore Deli
132 Crosby St. btwn. Houston & Prince

Don't expect décor, but do stop in any time you crave an honest cup of chai. Add an order of samosas, or rice with curried goat and vegetables for a cheap, filling meal.
• Daily 24 hours • Subway: B/D/F/V trains to Broadway-Lafayette; 6 train to Bleeker St. • Tel. 212-965-1777 • Cash only • Tea by the cup. Snacks. Entrees. $

MarieBelle Cacao Bar and Tea Room
484 Broome St. near West Broadway

This charming shop, named for designer and founder Maribel Leiberman, has delighted discriminating chocoholics and tea fans since October 2000. The front room is dominated by a stained-glass shop sign; antique furniture and glass cabinets are filled to the brim with custom confections, confiture,

and gift baskets. Eight romantically named, hand-blended teas, including Love's Labour Lychee and Blooming Heavens Chinese Flower, are beautifully packaged in turquoise and gold tins.

25

Luscious morsels, decorated with edible silk-screened graphics, are almost too pretty to eat. All are handmade using up to 72 percent cacao beans, fresh fruit essences, and rich creams. Over 20 flavors of chocolate are available, including Earl Grey tea, saffron, spices, cardamom, lemon, and hazelnut. MarieBelle is famous for hot chocolate powder in four signature flavors – Aztec Original, Dark, Mocha, and Spicy - made from the purest Belgian cocoa and highly refined sugars.

Walk past the line of loyal patrons, waiting to pay for their plunder at the front counter, to enter the cacao bar and tea room. Sample the shop's incredibly rich hot chocolate spiced with cinnamon, chipotle, and nutmeg or try a pot of Dark Obsession Chocolate Rose tea served with biscotti, decadent dark-chocolate brownies, and other sweet treats.

• Daily 11am-7pm • Subway: N/R/W trains to Prince St.; 6 train to Spring St. • Tel. 212-925-6999 • Major credit cards • www.mariebelle.com • Pot of tea. Sweets. Snacks. $

McNally Robinson Booksellers
52 Prince St. btwn. Mulberry & Lafayette Sts.

"Tea and books just seem to go together," says shop owner Sarah McNally, whose family owns several McNally Robinsons in Canada. This location is an independent book store located north of Little Italy in downtown Manhattan. A low-key café, walls painted a soothing sage green, hung with contemporary paintings, and furnished with hand-crafted copper-topped tables, provides a quiet place to enjoy a pot of tea and a snack.

Fellow Canadian, Kevin Gascoyne, supplies the fine quality tea from the company he

co-owns, Kyela. He trained the staff to brew loose leaves in black, cast-iron teapots delivered to the table with mini-hourglasses and slips of paper printed with enigmatic tea quotes. The menu features white tea, Chinese greens, Indian and Taiwanese oolongs, a Darjeeling from Avon-Grove, and Jin Zhen from Fujian. Celosia, a green leaf tea with jasmine and celosia flowers, is the best seller.

• Mon.-Sat. 10am-10pm, Sun. 10am-9pm • Subway: N/R/W trains to Prince St. • Tel. 212-274-1160 • Major credit cards • Pot of tea. Snacks. $

Pearl River Mart
477 Broadway btwn. Grand & Broom Sts.

Thirty years ago when there was no direct trade between China and the U.S., a group of young, Chinese-New Yorkers decided to open an American-style department store stocked with quality Chinese goods. It was an instant hit. Today, the great-wall-of-china includes teapot and cup sets for as little as $9.50 – blue and white willow ware, crackle glazes, lucky gold coin, gold-fish, and fortune cat designs. Loose tea is sold by the ounce or in decorative tins. There are aisles of boxed specialty tea bags – ginseng, dieter's and lover's tea (different formulas for women and men) as well as Asian and Western-style tea strain-ers and scoops. Climb the stairs to the balcony tea room for a pot of freshly brewed loose tea and a nibble. Refreshed, you're ready to choose a set of calligraphy tea paper party favors – 80 sheets for $3.50.

The "great wall of china" in the Pearl River Mart features teapots and cup sets at prices to please every shopper.

• Daily 10am-7:20pm • Subway: R/W trains to Prince St., 6 train to Spring St. • Tel. 212-431-4770 • Major credit cards • www.pearlriver.com • Pot of tea. $

Sweet Melissa Patisserie
75 W. Houston St. (corner W. Broadway)

French Culinary Institute graduate Melissa Murphy Hagenbart knows how to bake a fancy French tart, but also makes classic American desserts and gourmet granola. Her Brooklyn-baked pastries, sweets, and savories are sold in a jewel-box of a store for sidewalk snack-ing or to-go. Main listing page 95.

• Mon.-Thur. 7am-10pm, Fri. 7am-midnight, Sun. 8am-10pm • Sub-way: B/D/F/V trains to Broadway Lafayette, N/R/W to Prince St. • www.sweetmelissapatisserie.com • Tel. 347-594-2541 • Credit card minimum $10 • Tea by the cup. Snacks. Sweets. $

Greenwich Village

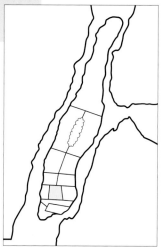

Native Americans camped and fished along the Minetta trout stream in a marshland that British colonists called *Grin'wich*. Next came farms, followed by aristocratic townhouses around Washington Square Park, home to artists, writers, and musicians including Edgar Allan Poe, Edith Wharton, Edward Hopper, Allen Ginsberg, and Bob Dylan. Today, the Village attracts college students, urbane professionals, actors, writers, and weekenders who love the vibrant atmosphere, well-preserved architecture, colorful shops, and tea hot spots.

Thé Adoré
17 East 13th St. btwn. University & 5th Ave.

Thé Adoré is a narrow slip of a shop with bakery counter take-out service on the first floor and table service up a short flight of stairs. Even on grey days, the space is cheerfully lit with light from the large windows overlooking the street.

Loose leaves from India, China, and Ceylon, including five types of Earl Grey, eleven blacks, as well as herbals are on offer. The menu also features a Continental-style breakfast of baguette, croissant, jam and tea. Sandwiches, salads, madeleines, soups, quiche, and other baked goods are always on offer. A small assortment of Mariage Fréres teas, teapots and brewing accoutrements are also for sale.

• Mon.-Fri. 8:30am-6:30 pm, Sat. 9am-5:30pm • Subway: 1/2/3 trains to 14th St. • Tel. 212-243-8742 • Cash only • Tea by the pot. Sandwiches. Soup. Sweets. $

Shopping Sites for Tea Lovers

Porto Rico Importing Co.
201 Bleeker St. btwn. MacDougal St. and 6th Ave.

The major business of the Porto Rico Importing company is coffee. However, the shop stocks more than 100 loose teas, as well as bagged teas from Benchley, Bewley, Fortnum and Mason, Tazo, and Twinings. Cast iron and ceramic teapots and brewing accessories are available. Second location in the East Village.
• Mon.-Sat. 9am-9pm. Sun. noon-7pm
• Major credit cards • Tel. 212-477-5421

Secrets of the Leaf
The tea plant, Camellia sinensis, grows as an evergreen shrub or tree that produces delicate flowers with five or seven white petals and bright yellow stamens. The bitter-tasting fruit is the size of a hazelnut and contains one to three seeds. Tea plants in a tea garden are plucked before they bloom.

29

West Village

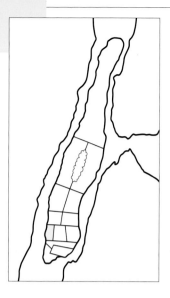

The **West Village,** bounded by Houston Street, 14th Street, Broadway, and the Hudson River, is an especially tolerant part of town, home to students and a large gay population.

Be-Speckled Trout
422 Hudson St. at St. Luke's Pl.

Anglers and Writers tearoom is no more, but the owner opened Be-Speckled Trout, a "candy café" and soda fountain right next door. A wooden canoe hangs from the tin ceiling. Antique fishing rods and other angling equipment are crammed in the tiny space, laid out like a country general store, with jars of penny candy, vintage tin signs, orphaned bone china cups and Brown Betty teapots. In addition to a real New York egg cream, you may order a chai latte at the two-seat soda fountain to sip with home-baked goods. A jam-filled sand-dollar cookie is just the ticket with tea.

• Mon.-Sat. 10am-8pm, Sun. 10am-7pm • Subway: 1 train to Houston St. • Tel. 212-255-1421 • Cash or check only • Tea by the cup. Sweets. $

Café Topsy
575 Hudson St. btwn. W. 11th and Bank Sts.

Café Topsy, named for the English owner's grandfather's donkey, "a discriminating eater," is just the place to sample authentic high tea fare on this side of the pond. This cheerful eatery doesn't take itself seriously, but they do deliver good British cooking. Come here for cottage pie (beef brisket cooked with vegetables topped with a mashed-potato crust), shepherd's pie (ground lamb and vegetables), fish and hand-cut chips (fries), English bangers and

Colcannon mash (pork sausages served over a potato-cabbage mix), or a Ploughman's lunch of English cheddar, Branston pickle, hard-boiled egg, bread, and a small salad. In Pursuit of Tea supplies the loose leaves, which are properly brewed and served in a ceramic Chatsford pot.

Café Topsy is named for the English owner's grandfather's donkey, "a discriminating eater."

• Tues.-Sat. 11am-10pm; Sun.-Mon. 5-9pm • Subway: A/C/E/L trains to 14th St. Walk south on 8th Ave. (turns into Hudson St.) • Tel. 646-638-2900 • Major credit cards • www.cafetopsy.com • Tea by the pot. Entrees and snacks. $

Cassava
474 6th Ave. btwn. 11th & 12th Sts.

This simple café offers free wireless internet access and serves eleven types of hot or cold bubble milk-tea made with loose-leaf black or green-jasmine tea. They also sell cupcakes and dessert bars.

• Mon.-Thurs. 8am-10pm, Fri. till midnight; Sat. noon-midnight; Sun. noon-10pm • Subway: F/V/L trains to 14th St. • Tel. 212-255-4805 • Credit card minimum $10 • www.cassavatea.com • Tea by the cup. Snacks and sweets. $

The Point Knitting Café
37A Bedford St. btwn. Carmine & Downing Sts.

Knit, sip, and be happy with a large cup of freshly brewed Mighty Leaf bag tea and a snack.

• Mon.-Fri. 8am-9pm, Sat.-Sun. 10am-7pm • Subway: A/C/E/F/B trains to West Fourth St. • Tel. 212-929-0800 • Major credit cards • Cup of tea. Snacks. $

Tea and Sympathy
108 Greenwich Ave. btwn. 12th & 13th Sts.

Tea & Sympathy is the cocky, cockney counterpart to the posh afternoon teas served in uptown hotels. The sign on the door warns that the staff is always right, and you won't be seated until your party is complete.

Nicola Perry, former London Stock Exchange tea lady, opened her ten-table tea room in 1990. It is beloved by Anglophiles and homesick Brits. Models, movie stars, airline crews and celebrity chefs – yes, that really is Ainsley Harriot of *Ready, Steady, Cook* fame seated at the corner table – come here to tuck into traditional comfort food such as cottage, shepherd and tweed-kettle pies, bangers and mash, Marmite on toast, Welsh rarebit, and puddings (cakes and trifles).

31

Assorted finger sandwiches, scones with clotted cream and strawberry or raspberry jam, and a selection of cakes and biscuits (cookies) are served on charmingly mismatched floral china. Taylors of Harrogate supplies fourteen types of loose tea; there's also the working man's favorite cuppa – Typhoo – and eight herbal infusions. Tea leaves will be left in the pot and "topped up" with hot water, English-style. God Save The Queen, Luv!

Next door, the **Carry On Tea & Sympathy Shop** is stocked with books, including *Tea and Sympathy: The Life of an English Tea Shop in New York*, British videos, groceries, teas, teapots, and accessories.

• Mon.-Sat. 11:30am-10:30pm, Sun. 11:30am-10pm • Subway: A/C/E trains to 14th St. at 8th Ave. • Tel. 212-989-9735 • Reservations not accepted • www.tea-andsympathynewyork.com • Major credit cards • Tea by the pot. Cream tea. Afternoon tea. $

Tea Spot
127 Macdougal St., corner of W. 3rd St.

This casual village internet café (free WiFi or LAN) offers a large number of teas for purchase by the ounce or to be consumed on site. Rooibos Chai, Masala Chai, decaffeinated Chai, bubble teas, and frozen tea lattes are popular with the student crowd. Light snacks, soups and sandwiches are also available. There are white, green, oolong and black loose teas from China, India, Japan, Nepal, Kenya, Sikkim and Taiwan, many organic choices, as well as herbal and fruit infusions such as yerba maté and pure Lapacho for sale. All teas are stored in huge tins conveniently labeled with name and description, but the server will be happy to let you sniff a sample.

• Mon.-Thurs. 8am-9pm, Fri.-Sat. 8am-11pm, Sun. 10am-7pm • Subway: A/B/C/D/E/F/V trains to W. 4th St. Washington Square • Tel. 212-832-7768 • Tea by the cup or pot. Snacks. Sweets. $

Yumcha
29 Bedford St., corner Bedford & Downing Sts.

At Yumcha ("to drink tea"), tea-infused salt and dried tea leaves are used to flavor modern Chinese haute cuisine such as tea-smoked chicken with a star anise infusion. Restaurateur JinR, chef and tea-blender at Beijing's Green T. House, created the exclusive blends including mingqian green tea with bamboo leaves. She recommends the

Forever Spring High Mountain Wulong as a post-dinner drink. If you sit at the sushi-style counter you can sip a green tea martini while watching Chef Angelo Sosa and staff scurry around the open kitchen. But it may get too smoky for comfort.

• Mon.-Sat. 6pm-midnight, Sun. 5-11pm • Subway: A/C/E/F/B trains to West Fourth St. • Tel. 212-524-6800 • Reservations required • www.yumchany.com • Major credit cards • Tea by the pot. Dim sum. Entrees. $$

Shopping Sites for Tea Lovers

Gourmet Garage
117 7th Ave S. btwn. Christopher & W. 10th Sts.

See flagship listing on page 82. • Daily 7am-10pm • Tel. 212-699-5980 • Subway: 1 train to Christopher St. • Major credit cards • www.gourmetgarage.com

McNulty's Tea & Coffee Company
109 Christopher St. btwn. Bleeker & Hudson Sts.

McNulty's has been located in the heart of Greenwich Village since 1895. The store still features a pressed tin ceiling, scales, and original bins stenciled with names of far away places. Oolongs, from Taiwan and China, including Shui Hsien Oolong ("Water Nymph"), blacks from Africa, China (Keemun, lapsang souchong, and Puerh), India, Russia, and Sri Lanka as well as a Young Hyson, Bancha, Pio Lo Chun and White Flowery Pekoe, are stored in glass jars, and available by mail order. The shop also stocks Jackson's of Piccadilly, Twinings, Williamson & Magor, Barry's, and Lyons & McGraths's of Ireland teas, along with teapots and brewing equipment.
• Closed Tues. Open Mon. and Wed.-Sat. 10am- 9pm, Sun. 1-7pm • Tel. 212-242-5351• Subway: 1 train to Christopher St. • www.mcnultys.com • Major credit cards

Located in Greenwich Village since 1895, McNulty's features a pressed tin ceiling, scales, and original bins stenciled with names of far away places.

Myers of Keswick
634 Hudson St. btwn. Horatio and Jane Sts.

Peter Myers grew up in Keswick, England. His family still runs a butcher shop there, famous for its Cumberland sausages. Myers arrived in New York in 1972 and worked as a bartender before discovering that British ex-pats (there are some 250,000 in the tri-state area) were hungry for food that reminded them of home. Freshly-made bangers, sausage rolls, pasties, pork pies, and other savory high tea treats are sold in Myers' shop, along with traditional British sweets, sauces, jams, curds, and condiments. The store stocks a dozen Taylors of Harrogate loose teas, as well as bagged selections from PG Tips, Twinings, and Typhoo.
• Mon.-Fri. 10am-7pm, Sat. 10am- 6pm, Sun. noon- 5pm • Subway: A/C/E to the 14th St. and 8th Ave. station. • Tel. 212-691-4194 • www.myersofkeswick.com

Peter Myers opened his West Village shop after discovering that British ex-pats were hungry for food that reminded them of home.

The Porcelain Room
13 Christopher St. btwn. 6th and 7th Aves.

Named after the porcelain room 18th-century European rulers filled with "White Gold," this shop is a treasure trove of antique European and Asian ceramics as well as contemporary hand-painted pieces made from the original molds.
• Daily noon-8pm • Subway: 1 train to Christopher St. A/C/E/F/B/D/Q to West 4th St. • Tel. 212-367-8206 • Major credit cards • www.theporcelainroom.com

William-Wayne and Company
40 University Pl. btwn. 9th and 10th Sts.

Vintage and contemporary tableware and linens. See main listing page 85.
• Mon.-Sat. 11am-7pm, Sun. 1- 6pm • Subway: 4/5/6/Q/N/R/W to Union Square 14th St. • Tel. 212-533-4711

Secrets of the Leaf
Orange Pekoe is a leaf grade and has nothing to do with citrus fruit. The exceptional grade was named in honor of the Dutch Monarchy, the House of Orange, by early Dutch traders.

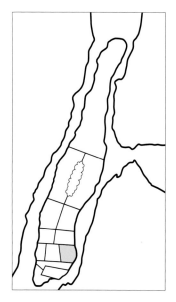

East Village

Punk music was born in the neighborhood some still consider part of the Lower East Side. In the 19th century, Astors and Vanderbilts lived east of Broadway. Today, the **East Village** is home to Yuppies, young Japanese, and older Eastern European immigrants.

Danal
90 E. 10th St. btwn. Third and Fourth Aves.

Afternoon tea is served on the second floor of this French-country bistro. Cheery yellow walls, a non-working fireplace, oriental rugs, and mismatched wooden furniture contribute to a charming, shabby-chic setting. Forty kinds of loose tea are available brewed in a Brown Betty teapot. Three types of tea sandwiches, two warm scones, Devon cream and preserves, and two slices of tea cake or tart are offered for a set tea. Service can be quirky. This is not the location for a large group.

• Afternoon tea served Fri.-Sat. 4-6pm
• Subway: 6 train to Astor Place, N/R trains to Broadway at 8th St. • Tel. 212-982-6930 • Reservations required • Child friendly • Major credit cards • Tea by the pot. Afternoon tea. $

Jenny's Café
113 St. Mark's Place (8th St.) btwn. 1st Ave. & Ave. A

Jenny's is a Pan-Asian & Pacific Rim/Japanese café with an extensive tea menu. She serves black, green, and oolong teas, as well as ten types of hot or cold milk-teas including papaya, black sesame, almond, and peanut. Thirteen green teas are offered. Her green tea smoothie is popular, as is the matcha milk tea, thought to be good for a bad cold. Other house specials are brown-rice tea, homemade honey-lemon-green tea, taro, almond, and coconut tea. Hot teas are served in a glass pot warmed by a tea candle. For dessert, sample the steamed green tea cake with green apple syrup.

St. Mark's-in-the-Bowery Church, which began as the Stuyvesant family's private chapel, is located two blocks north of Jenny's Cafe.

• Mon.-Thurs. and Sun. 1pm-midnight, Fri.-Sat. 1pm-2am • Subway: 6 train to Astor Place • Tel. 212-674-4739 • Cash only • Tea by the cup or pot. Snacks. $

Knit New York
307 E. 14th St. btwn. 1st & 2nd Aves.

Knitters, male and female, may enjoy a cup of freshly brewed loose tea (fifteen Serendipitea selections) and a sweet or savory snack, while casting on.
• Café open Mon.-Fri. 8am-8pm, Sat -Sun. 9am-8pm • Subway: L/N/Q/R/W/4/5/6 trains to 14th St. Union Square (knit shop open 10am-8pm) • Tel. 212-387-0707 • Major credit cards • www.knitnewyork.com • Cup of tea. Snacks. $

Podunk
231 E. 5th St. btwn. 2nd & 3rd Aves.

Minnesota native Elspeth Treadwell is on a mission to make tea less froufrou. At Podunk, her tiny tea room, the feeling is casual. There's no table service and no tipping, just lots of good, old-fashioned baking and delicious tea. Pitchers of herb and fruit-flavored iced tea are available, along with hot-tea punches, homemade chai, thirty-five loose teas, and a dozen Podunk custom blends including organic sage-sencha, vanilla-coconut black, and full-bodied teas such as osmanthus oolong, plus herbals, tisanes, and hot chocolate infused with flavored teas.

Ms. Treadwell presents seventeen imaginative set-tea menus informally served on mismatched china plunked on a wooden tray. Among them is *The Blunt and Savory Tea*: three mini-tea pies (French-onion, chicken, ham with gorgonzola cheese and cranberry), sweet and savory scones, and peppery cheese biscuits. Sweets include Scandinavian specialties – cardamom ring and sticky buns, as well as American classics such as cookie bars, cupcakes, shortbread, sugar cookies, and butter-cream layer cake – the kind you wished your mother could bake. Everything is made to-order, so pluck a copy of *Charlotte's Web* from the bookcase and settle back in your Adirondack chair.

(continued on page 38)

Cha-An

230 E 9th St. btwn. 2nd & 3rd Aves.

You don't have to travel to Tokyo to experience a traditional Japanese-style tea, but you do have to climb two flights of stairs to reach Cha-An ("little place to have tea"). The restaurant's bustling open kitchen and bar are balanced by a traditional, three-tatami-mat tea room roofed with bamboo. A bed of river pebbles winds to a low stone basin where guests, who have booked the tea room for a *cha-no-yu* demonstration, stoop to wash their hands and remove shoes.

Cha-An serves a Western-style afternoon tea prepared with great care and creativity by executive chef Tomoko Kato, a young Japanese woman. Three set teas, a sweets tea, and the chef's dessert-of-the-day assortment, served with a pot of tea, are available. The savories include tea-smoked salmon, a soy-milk-mushroom quiche, and five-grain rice. The black sesame crème brulee and green-tea truffles, shaped like miniature cabbages, are sure to delight.

The extensive tea menu, supplied by Brooklyn's In Pursuit of Tea, offers seven types of green tea, two whites, two Puerhs, six blacks, three oolongs, and nine herbals, including an Assam from the Meleng Estate, a Second Flush Goomtee Darjeeling, and Keemun Mao Feng. Everybody knows that you can't make good tea without good water, so Cha-An imported a $5,000 Japanese water filter for better brewing.

• Daily noon-5pm • Subway: N/R/Q/W trains to 8th St., 6 train to Astor Place • Tel. 212-228-8030 • Reservations required • Cash only • www.cha-an.com • Afternoon set tea. $$

Secrets of the Leaf
Japanese tea is grown in hill country near rivers, streams, and lakes where hot sunshine is tempered by damp mist.

• Closed Mondays. Open: Tues.-Sun. 11am-9pm • Subway: 6 train to Astor Place • Tel. 212-677-7722 • Reservations not accepted • Cash or check only • Tea by the pot. Informal set tea. Sweets. Savories. $$

St. Alp's Teahouse
39 Third Ave. btwn. 9th & 10th Sts.

This Hong Kong-based chain is named for the Chinese saint who left an imprint of his foot on a rock in Northern Taipei. The no-frills décor nods East with Chinese-style dark wood tables and stools. The place hums at all hours with NYU students, young families, and creative types in colorful clothing. St. Alp's prides itself on serving genuine Taiwanese frothy tea with pearl tapioca. Their pearls are made with premium tea leaves and starch extracted from sweet potatoes and cassava root combined with brown sugar. There are eleven refreshing flavors including almond, coconut, peanut, taro, and sesame. The Classical series presents a variety of black teas with fruit flavors and iced, roasted Ti Kwan Yin or Oolong. In addition to jasmine green tea, there are seven fruit-herb blends, as well as milk shakes. Light refreshments include lemon tea jelly, toast with green tea butter, and flavored tea eggs.

• Mon.-Thurs. noon-midnight, Fri.-Sat. noon-1am, Sun. 1pm-11pm • Subway: 6 train to Astor Place • Tel. 212-598-1890 • Cash only • Tea by the cup. Snacks. $

Sympathy for the Kettle
109 St. Mark's Pl. (8th St.) btwn. First Ave. & Ave. A

Jodi Holiday moved to the East Village after completing graduate school in Boston. Employed in publishing and finance, Ms. Holiday took a permanent holiday from corporate America to open her own business. She designed Sympathy for the Kettle, a riff on a Rolling Stone lyric, to attract young students and artists who live in the neighborhood. Rose pink curtains frame the window; the brick walls are painted lavender. "I wanted to make tea colorful, fun, exciting, and affordable. I convert coffee-drinkers everyday with matcha tea lattes steeped in milk and honey."

Jodi buys her teas from small, family-owned estates. She offers organic and fair trade options whenever possible. The shop has thirty-five classic teas such as Earl Grey, first and second-flush Darjeelings, oolongs, Assam, and Puerh, as well as a large assortment of greens, seven types of white teas, seven chai blends, Rooibos, maté, and

East 9th Street between Second Avenue and Avenue A is one of the city's hippest shopping strips. There are boutiques for fashionable and ethnic clothing, home furnishings, and gifts.

other herbal-fruit infusions. Up to 150 types of loose tea may be special ordered.

Local farmers and bakers supply honey and sweet and savory treats – vanilla-Rooibos cake, lavender-tea truffles, spinach and arugula sandwiches – to be enjoyed with a pot of tea at one of the shop's five tables or packed to-go. Asian and Western-style teapots and accessories are also for sale. Ms. Holiday books special events for up to twenty tea lovers, and she caters events at outside locations.

• Closed Mondays. Open daily 11am-11pm • Tel. 212-979-1650 • Major credit cards • Subway: 6 train to Astor Place • Tea by the pot or cup. Snacks. Sweets. • www.sympathyforthekettle.com $

Tsampa
212 E 9th St. btwn. 2nd & 3rd Aves.

Tsampa is a family-run, natural foods restaurant with a menu drawn from the hearty, spicy cuisines of Tibet, Nepal, China, India, and Bhutan. Waitresses wearing traditional dark blue Tibetan dress, bright striped aprons, and high-topped sneakers are part of the cross-cultural experience. Numerous photos of the Dalai Lama, the religious and political leader of exiled Tibetans, preside over the serene space. Try to sit in the back where the glimpse of a trellised Buddhist garden makes New York seem far, far away.

A bowl of salty, buttery, black bocha tea and an order of steamed or fried vegetable dumplings, called momos, served with red or green hot sauce, will warm you up on a frosty night. Chai, hot or cold, is delicious with the Tsampa dessert – traditional Tibetan roasted ground barley fluffed with yogurt and honey dotted with dried cranberries. They serve a very good green tea ice cream.

• Daily 5-11:30pm • Subway: N/R/Q/W trains to 8th St., 6 train to Astor Place • Tel. 212-614-3226 • Major credit cards • Pot of bocha. Chai. Momos. Crepes. Sweets. $

Porto Rico Importing Co.
40 1/2 St. Mark's Pl. btwn. 1st & 2nd Aves.

Coffee, loose teas, and teaware. Additional location in Greenwich Village; see main listing on page 29.
• Mon.-Sat. 9am-9pm. Sun. noon-7pm • Tel. 212- 533-1982 • Major credit cards

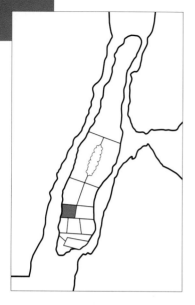

Chelsea

and the Meat Packing District

In Chelsea and the old Meat Packing District, industrial buildings have been gutted and reborn as luxury lofts, designer shops, trendy bars, and art galleries.

Belgian Chocolates
English Fine Foods
Gift Hampers
Corporate Gifts
Imported Teas
Delivery/Shipping

Bodum Café and Homestore
413-415 W.14th St. btwn. 9th & 10th Sts.

Bodum stocks over 100 loose leaf teas – basics, blends, and better quality self-drinkers from China, India, Japan, Java, Kenya and Nepal, as well as Rooibos and herbal-fruit infusions. Each tea is merchandized with a tasting tin so that you can see and smell a sample before purchase. Or take the sample to the café bar where a cup will be brewed for a minimal charge. Catered by Aquavit Restaurant and Sarabeth's, snacks include sandwiches, sweets and salads served with a pot of freshly pressed tea.

ASSAM TEAPOT

bodum

• Café open daily 10am-7pm • Subway: A/C/E/L trains to 14th St. Station at 8th Ave. • Tel. 212-367-9125 • Major credit cards • www.bodumusa.com • Tea by pot or cup. Snacks. $

Lobby Café at the Rubin Museum of Art
150 West 17th St., East of 7th Ave.

The Rubin Museum of Art, which opened in 2004, houses one of the world's largest collections of Himalayan art, drawn primarily from India, southwest China, Nepal, Bhutan, and Burma, dating from the 12th through 19th centuries.

The sidewalk entrance leads to a large room containing the café and gift shop. A ceiling made of translucent fabric vaults over a parade of mosaic-rimmed columns. Sage-green walls are hung with colorful photographs of Tibetan landscapes and Buddhist festivals. The sound of softly chanting monks fills the space set with twenty delicate wooden tables and chairs.

On the left, a 30-foot counter displays sandwiches, salads, soups, and desserts. Each dish is presented as a work of art on a colorful mat or tiered server. There are Wasabi-spiked tuna salad sandwiches served on seven-grain bread, green tea wasabi peanuts, and an Asian chef salad composed of greens, red curry shrimp, grilled chicken, peanuts, raisins, toasted coconut, and mandarin oranges drizzled with miso vinaigrette. Grilled panini and a soup of the day also are available.

Chocolate lovers will rave about the Naga "haut chocolat" candy bars with exotic ingredients – Japanese ginger, wasabi, and black sesame seeds. Curry sugar cookies, silk-screened with an image from the collection, are an unusual accent for gelato, sorbet, or yogurt fruit smoothies.

The tea menu offers In Pursuit of Tea White Peony, Jasmine Pearls, Nantou Oolong, Assam, First Flush Darjeeling, Earl Grey,

41

Puerh ("the base tea used in Tibetan Yak Butter Tea"), a delicious herbal cardamom chai, lemon verbena and a Scarlet Glow iced tea made with lemon verbena, elderflower, milk thistle, and hibiscus. The loose tea is brewed by the cup (biodegradable paper) in a disposable tea sack. Packaged tea is sold in the gift shop along with yeti-appliqué pillows and a wonderful collection of books, scarves and jewelry.

• Closed Mon. Open other days 11am. Closing times: Tues. and Sat. 7pm, Wed. 5pm, Thurs.-Fri. 9pm, Sun. 6pm • Subway: 1 train to 18th St., 7th Ave. • Tel. 212-620-5000 • www.rmanyc.org • Tea by the cup. Snacks. Sweets. $

Nicole Farhi 202 Bistro Café
75 Ninth Ave., at 16th St. next door to Chelsea Market

Designer Nicole Farhi's Midtown location no longer serves afternoon tea, but her latest venture, a bistro café, named for its London counterpart, serves tea and English-style baked goods daily. **202** is two-thirds cozy restaurant and wine bar, with one-third devoted to retail featuring housewares, furniture, and elegant fashions.

Chef Annie Wayte prepares a different menu every day based on what's fresh in the market. Tea treats might include ginger scones with homemade jam, jam brioche buns, blackberry or zucchini-walnut muffins, almond-cherry macaroons, banana bread, olive-oil cake with strawberries and cream, luscious lemon bars, and chocolate macadamia whoppers. A dozen loose teas from QI Botanical, a Canadian company, are brewed by the pot.

• Afternoon tea served daily 4-5:30pm • Subway: A/C/E/L trains to 14th St. Station at 8th Ave. • Tel. 646-638-0115 • www.nicolefarhi.com

Shopping Sites for Tea Lovers

Chelsea Market Baskets (in Chelsea Market)
75 Ninth Ave., btwn. 15th & 16th Sts.

Once a Nabisco cookie-factory, the block-long Chelsea Market is now a chic place to shop for gourmet groceries and specialty items. You may buy beautifully packaged bagged tea, English and European epicurean treats, and custom gift baskets at the Chelsea Market Baskets store.
• Mon.-Fri. 9:30am-7:30pm, Sat. 10am-7:30pm, Sun. 10am-6pm • Subway: A/C/E/L trains to 14th St. Station at 8th Ave. • Tel. 212-727-1111 • Major credit cards • www.chelseamarketbaskets.com

Some of New York's most fashionable shopping and living spaces have been created from former industrial buildings. Chelsea Market, once an eight-story cookie factory, is home to The Food Network, Sarabeth's bakery, an Italian market, florist, butcher, wine shop, kitchen store and lots of fun eateries.

Wild Lily Tea Room
511-A West 22nd St. btwn.10th and 11th Aves.

Guests at this Asian-fusion tea room are greeted by the soothing sound of water gurgling in a circular fishpond set in the multilevel floor. If you're seated by the pond, look for the ornamental goldfish gliding in the depths.

Tea fans will be spoiled for choice with over 40 connoisseur-grade teas from China, India, Taiwan, and Japan including Buddha's Finger (loose leaves rolled to resemble the sacred digit), first and second-flush single-estate Darjeelings, and fun teas (green tea with popcorn kernels). Uptown Eve and Chelsea Adam are among the restorative herbal tonics.

The Afternoon Tea Party menu is presented on a three-tiered server with lily pad-shaped plates. Some of the English-style tea sandwiches are made with an Asian sensibility - Chinese black tea egg salad, ginger-poached chicken with curry sauce on French bread, cucumber with rice-vinegar-honey sauce, and a delicious butternut squash cream spread on walnut-raisin bread. Freshly made apricot-almond scones are served with clotted cream and homemade jam. There's a variety of cookies and a daily cake special. Green tea fans will be delighted with many desserts – green tea mille crepe, green tea tiramisu, green tea pound cake, and green tea mochi ice cream.

The tea room sells a variety of loose teas as well as contemporary and traditionally-styled ceramic, glass, and metal teapots. Check their web site for green tea stationery and green tea tissues. Seasonal tea tastings, demonstrations, and a tea club membership are available.

• Closed Mon. Other days: "Afternoon Tea Party" served 2-5pm • Subway: C/E/1/9 trains to 23rd St. • Tel. 212-691-2258 • Reservations required • Major credit cards • www.wildlilytearoom.com • Tea by the pot. Full afternoon tea. $$

Whole Foods Market
250 7th Avenue at 24th St.

Loose and bagged tea, teapots, and tea treats. See flagship listing on page 93.
• Daily 8am-10pm • Subway: 1 train to 23rd St. • Tel. 212-924-5969 • Major credit cards • www.wholefoodsmarket.com

Secrets of the Leaf

India is the world's largest producer of organic tea. More than a million people, 60 percent of whom are female, work on 25,000 gardens of various sizes. A skilled female plucker can harvest 82 pounds of green leaves a day – 44 pounds of processed tea. Read more about Indian tea traditions on page 51.

Gramercy Park, Kips Bay and Union Square

Visitors to the neighborhoods southeast of Midtown will discover tea traditions from Afghanistan, India, and Thailand as well as charming spots for an English-style afternoon tea. Originally a "crooked little swamp," **Gramercy Park** was drained in 1831, and the surrounding streets were laid out to emulate elite London squares. **Kips Bay**, also known as Little India, offers many places to sample *chai*, a popular form of tea, and *mithai*, sweets. **Union Square**, in the shadow of the **Flatiron District,** is home to a Greenmarket, overflowing with farm-fresh produce.

Bamiyan Afghani Restaurant
358 Third Ave., corner of 26th St.

Bamiyan Afghani Restaurant, named after the cultural heart of Afghanistan, was established in 1966. Sayed Ahmad Shah, the restaurant's host and co-owner, a Supreme Court Justice in his homeland, was visiting New York when Russia invaded Afghanistan. Unable to return home, Mr. Shah, who loved to cook, became a restaurateur.

For centuries, caravans traveling the Silk Road rested in Afghanistan. Bamiyan's menu reflects elements of Chinese, Greek, Indian, and Turkish cuisine. Afghanistan is famous for its grilled-meat kabobs, but you could make a delicious afternoon tea with several savory appetizers – *aushak* (steamed scallion dumplings), *dolma* (ground beef and rice wrapped in grape leaves), and *boulanee kadu* (pumpkin turnover spiced with cinnamon and cloves, served with mint-yogurt dip). For high tea add a salad of cucumbers, scallions, tomatoes, and mint leaves, plus a pasta, vegetarian, or meat entrée. Desserts include *baklava*, *phirnee* (pistachio and rose-water pudding), and *goosh-e fil* (fried dough elephant ears).

Afghani chai, called *shir-chay*, traditionally made with cardamom, saffron, green tea, rose petals, and milk, is much lighter than the Indian version. The restaurant also offers Darjeeling, Earl Grey, Persian tea, green tea, cardamom, mint tea, and herbal infusions. Seated at a low table on carpet-covered cushions, surrounded by decorative objects straight from the bazaar, you'll feel like you're having an adventure.

• Daily noon-11pm • Subway: N/R train to 28th St. • Tel. 212-481-3232 • Major credit cards • www.bamiyan.com • Tea by the pot or cup. Entrées. Sweets. Snacks. $

Keko Café Gourmet Coffee and Tea House
121 Madison Ave. at 30th St.

Keko does a bustling take-out and gourmet gift basket business, but customers may sit at one of the ten small tables to enjoy a pot of freshly brewed Harney's loose tea. Tea time here is a very casual affair. The a la carte selections are more interesting, and the breakfast crepes would make savory or sweet tea snacks. There are delicious baked goods: scones, croissants, *pain au chocolat*, brioche, baklava, mango as well as lemon squares, and assorted fancy cakes.

• Mon.-Fri. 7am-8pm, afternoon tea served 2:30-6pm • Tel. 212-685-4360 • Reservations not accepted • Major credit cards • Tea by the pot or cup. Snacks. Sweets. $

Visitors to the area surrounding Gramercy Park may enjoy a visit to Theodore Roosevelt's Birthplace, The National Arts Club, and The Players Club.

Kelley and Ping
340 3rd Ave. at 25th St

Kelley and Ping is a combination tea shop, Asian grocery, and noodle bar offering two dozen freshly brewed teas and Thai iced tea. Fourteen types of loose tea are for sale including Chrysanthemum, Gen Mai Cha, Gunpowder and Iron Goddess of Mercy, Lotus, Lemon, Spice and Vanilla. Second location in Soho; see listing on page 25.

• Daily 11:30am-11pm • Subway: R/W/6 trains to 23rd St. • Tel 212-871-7000 • Major credit cards • www.kelleyandping.com • Tea by the pot or cup. A la carte menu. $

Madras Mahal
104 Lexington Ave. btwn. 27th & 28th Sts.

Opened in 1983, Madras Mahal is New York's first kosher-vegetarian Indian restaurant. It features food from South and North India. Although they don't serve afternoon tea, visit at tea time to snack on appetizers, sweets, and milky Masala chai steeped with spices. *Dosas*, thin crepes, or *uttapas*, pancakes, are delicious South Indian street-snacks. *Gulab jamu*, sweet cheese balls swimming in syrup, accompanied by mango ice cream, would be wonderful with Assam tea.

• Mon.-Fri. 11:30am-3pm and 5-10pm., Sat.-Sun. noon-10pm • Subway: 6 train to 28th St. • Tel. 212-684-4010 • Major credit cards • Tea by the cup. Tea snacks and sweets. $

T Salon and T Emporium
11 E. 20th St. btwn. Broadway and Fifth Ave.

This high-energy temple to tea is an artful blend of Asian mysticism steeped in New York attitude. Guests might find themselves seated next to a spiritualist reading fortunes, a celebrity seeking anonymity, or a couple of tired tourists in search of a really good cup of tea.

Owner Miriam Novalle, a former fragrance designer, creates exotic custom blends with names such as Sunrise in Tibet, Whispering Heaven, and Tibetan Tiger. Enjoy a pot of tea with scones or lunch.

The two-floor T Emporium carries a full line of tea accoutrements and one of the city's most complete selections of outstanding single estate teas, blended teas, and fruit or herbal tisanes.

• Mon.-Sat. 10am-8pm, Sun. 11am-7pm • Subway: N/R/V/F/6 trains to 23rd St. • Tel. 212-358-0506 • Major credit cards • www.tsalon.com • Tea by the pot. Full set afternoon tea. $$

The townhouses skirting Gramercy Park were designed by some of New York's best architects and sheltered Teddy Roosevelt and other prominent citizens. Even today, only those lucky few whose windows overlook the leafy square own a key to the two-acre fenced park.

47

Lady Mendl's Tea Salon at the Inn at Irving Place
56 W. Irving Pl. btwn. 17th and 18th Sts.

In 1834, three single-family brownstones sat at the corner of 17th Street and Irving Place. The two remaining houses, meticulously restored, create The Inn. You'll need to look carefully for the discreet brass plaque bearing the name *Lady Mendl's*.

Lady Mendl's Tea Salon is named for Elsie DeWolfe, the flamboyant socialite, actress, interior designer, and World War I nurse who once lived across the street. After a long relationship with Elisabeth Marbury, a literary agent and producer, Elsie shocked society again, at age sixty, by marrying British diplomat Sir Charles Mendl, and acquiring the title, Lady Mendl.

This salon is consistently rated one of the most romantic places to enjoy tea in the city. Victorian-style architecture, period antique furniture, and art recreate a time of sublime elegance. Small tables draped with white, lacy linens are scattered throughout two first-floor rooms. Guests may also elect to sit on sofas in front of the fireplace. The Evelyn Nesbitt or Marbury Room may be booked in advance for larger groups and special functions.

The sumptuous five-course tea is successively served in a leisurely fashion. The meal includes a mixed green salad, a variety of finger sandwiches (smoked salmon with dill-cream cheese on pumpernickel, cucumber with mint-crème fraiche on brioche, goat cheese and sun-dried tomato on seven-grain bread, and smoked turkey and cranberry on brioche), freshly baked scones with Devonshire cream and preserves, cake, assorted cookies, chocolate-covered strawberries, and a large selection of teas.

Due to the successive nature of the service, Lady Mendel's expects guests to be prompt. A 15-minute grace period is allowed for reservations.

• Five-course tea served Wed.-Fri. at 3pm or 5pm, Sat.-Sun. at 2pm or 4:30pm • Subway: L/N/Q/R/W/4/5/6 trains to 14th St. Union Sq.
• Tel. 212-533-4466 • Reservations required one month in advance
• Major credit cards • www.LadyMendls.com • Full afternoon tea. $$

Tamarind Tea Room
41-43 East 22nd St. btwn. Broadway & Park Ave. South

A sweet-sour fruit used to flavor chutney, curry, and other Indian dishes gives its the name to this sophisticated tea room. The sleek space, decorated in grey and sage, only seats eleven, but tea may also be ordered in the restaurant next door. Fourteen loose-leaf teas from India, China, Japan, Sri Lanka, and Taiwan are offered along with an herbal chai and flower-herb tisanes. The menu, a culinary journey through India, suggests a tea to compliment each item. Dunk your cake rusks, a bit like biscotti, in Masala

chai. Drink Darjeeling with *nan khatai*, spiced lentil shortbread, or the tomato-tamarind sandwich wrap. Ti Kuan Yin tea is superb with the *ajwain* biscuit, an addictive, sweet-salty cookie with a faint fennel flavor. Assam is strong enough to stand up to the assertive flavors of the lamb *sholley* streaked with mint-yogurt dressing. Delicate tarts, scones, muffins, and pound cake are paired with greens and herbal infusions. Ask your server for the daily special and additional tea recommendations.

• Daily 11:30am-3pm, Sun.-Thurs. 5:30-11:30pm, Fri.-Sat. 5pm-midnight • Subway: 6 train to 23rd St. • Tel. 212-674-7400 • Reservations recommended • Major credit cards • www.tamarinde22.com • Tea by the pot. Sandwiches. Sweets. $

Tibetan Kitchen
444 Third Ave at 31st St.

Centuries ago, the Chinese compressed tea leaves into bricks to make them easy to transport along the Silk Road. Tibetans traded wool for tea and soaked crumbled bricks overnight in water. Next day, the infused tea was churned in a wooden *jhandong* with salt, yak butter, and goat milk. This broth-like brew, called *bocha*, fortified moun-

tain dwellers against the fierce cold. When the cup was drained, the butter residue was rubbed into chapped skin. Today, Tibetans produce an organic green tea; they also drink black Nepalese tea and Puerh. Tea is known as "the water of long life," consumed on a daily basis and often served with *momos*, steamed dumplings or buns. The bocha at the Tibetan Kitchen is delicious on a cold night with Tibetan chicken curry or *sha momo*, beef and vegetable dumplings. *Bhaktsa markhoo*, a dessert pasta made with tsampa flour, brown sugar and grated cheese, is tasty with chai.

• Mon-Fri. noon-3pm, 5-11pm, Sat.-Sun. 2-11pm • Subway: 6 train to 33rd St. • Tel. 212-679-6286 • Major credit cards • Tea by the cup. Entrees. Snacks. $

Shopping Sites for Tea Lovers

Spice Corner
135 Lexington Ave. at 29th St.
Sweets and tea treats with a touch of India.
• Daily 10am-8pm • Subway: 6 train to 28th St. • Tel. 212-689-5182 • Major credit cards

Whole Foods Market
4 Union Square South

New York has three Whole Foods Markets; all are enormous and well organized. Speciality loose tea supplied by Rishi and In Pursuit of Tea (properly packaged in light and air-tight containers) is sold in the coffee department along with Bee House teapots and ceramic storage jars. Kusmi and Taylors of Harrogate loose teas are stocked, along with bagged Bigelow, Numi, Republic of Tea, Twinings, Zhena's Gypsy Tea, Oregon chai mix, and several herbal brands. While you're here, load up on freshly baked breads and pastries, jams, honey, and condiments for your next tea party. (Additional locations in Chelsea and Upper West Side.)

• Daily 8am-10pm • Subway: L/N/Q/R/W/4/5/6 train to 14th St. Union Square • Tel. 212-673-5388 • Major credit cards • www.wholefoodsmarket.com

Tibetan Kitchen, which claims to be America's first Tibetan restaurant, serves buttered and salted bocha as well as hot chai made with Darjeeling tea.

In Tibetan monasteries, novices are responsible for preparing tea and serving it to monks while they pray. Lamas hold a morning prayer ceremony at which tsampa (roasted barley) is combined with tea. The porridge is sanctified and served as a holy tea offering.

Indian Tea Traditions

For centuries, tea was cultivated as a medicinal stimulant by indigenous tribes living in Assam, a region of northeast India. In the early 19th century, the British were looking for a place outside China to grow tea. Bessa Gaum, chief of the Singhpo tribe, graciously gave native tea seeds to Robert Bruce, a Scottish adventurer and trader, in 1823. Bruce's brother successfully cultivated the Assam plant, and by 1838 London Tea Auctions declared Indian tea to be as good as, if not better than, Chinese.

Today, India is the world's largest producer of organic tea. The nation's best-known teas are robust, malty Assam; Darjeeling, the champagne of Indian teas prized for its muscatel flavor; and brisk, bright Nilgiri from Southern India's Blue Mountains. Kashmiri people drink green tea, sometimes flavored with crushed almonds and cardamom. But *chai*, (rhymes with *pie* – a drink made with ground black tea infused with milk, sugar, and a variety of spices) is India's national drink. Chai is brewed everywhere, all day and into the night. Peddlers (*chai wallas*) stand on streets, steaming kettles in hand, poised to fill a glass or disposable pottery cup.

The British introduced afternoon tea during the Victorian era, and it is traditionally served at four o'clock. In Assam, fresh tea leaves dipped in batter and deep-fried make a tasty savory with a cup of milky tea. In New York, savories and sweet confections are sold at Indian bakeries and restaurants to enjoy with a casual cup of chai.

Ask any Indian living in New York the best place to drink chai and the answer is always: "My mother's house." However, cabbies swear by the chai at the Lahore Deli, a tiny hole-in-the wall. The most sophisticated Indian afternoon tea is served at Tamarind.

Secrets of the Leaf

Darjeeling, one of the best-known names in tea, comes only from the 86 tea gardens found in the Darjeeling area of northern India. First Flush and Second Flush Darjeelings are the first and second pickings of the year. They are the perfect accompaniment to any afternoon tea.

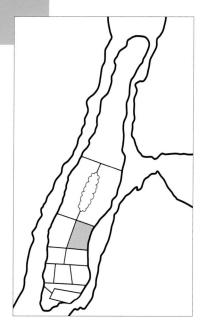

Midtown East

Midtown East is famous for shopping, luxury hotels, and tourist attractions such as the Empire State Building and the United Nations. You can't really breakfast at Tiffany's, but you can sip a calming cuppa presented with English, French, Japanese, Korean, or Lebanese flair in this neighborhood.

American Girl Café
609 Fifth Ave., corner 49th St.

A day at American Girl Place, an enormous three-story store, is a dream come true for young readers who love Kit, Samantha, and the rest of the characters in *The American Girls Collection* books. At the third floor cafe, girls delight in afternoon tea served in a whimsical black-and-white setting. Dolls are invited to sit at the table in little high chairs. Conversation-starter questions, placed in a gift-box on each table, prompt girls to tell stories and share memories.

SUBMITTED PHOTO

The menu includes "girl-friendly" foods named after American Girl characters – Kirsten's chocolate chip scones with marshmallow cream and candy fruit wedges; Josefina's tomato boats with star-shaped chicken-salad sandwiches. Sweet surprises, including a chocolate tea cup, complete the meal. Beverages include cocoa, coffee, iced tea, milk, pink lemonade, or a pot of tea brewed with two bags. Group packages are available for parties.

• Afternoon tea served daily 4-5pm • Subway: E/V trains to Fifth Ave., B/D/F/V to 47th-50th Sts. at Rockefeller Ctr. • Tel. 877-247-5223 • Reservations required at least a month in advance • Child friendly • Major credit cards • www.americangirl.com • Full afternoon set tea. $$

Café Opaline, Dahesh Museum of Art
580 Madison Ave. btwn. 56th and 57th Sts.

Lebanese author and philosopher, Salim Moussa Achi (Dr. Dahesh) collected 19th and 20th-century European academic art. Dahesh hoped to house the collection in a museum in his native Beirut, but civil war drove it to the United States. The Dahesh Museum of Art opened in 1995, showcasing long forgotten academic themes – the Bible, ancient myths, literature, and the exotic Orient. In 2003, the growing museum moved into its current location.

SUBMITTED PHOTO

You need not visit the Museum's galleries to enjoy a meal at Café Opaline; simply take the elevator two levels up to the restaurant. Arrange to sit in the corner where two floor-to-ceiling windows meet and jut out, like the prow of a ship, sailing serenely over the bustling street below. Although the ambiance is sleek and contemporary, the table is set with a damask cloth and generously-sized napkins.

In Pursuit of Tea supplies a dozen loose-leaf choices – greens, blacks, blends and herbal tisanes – served in individual pots with a strainer. A pot of hot water is provided to dilute the second steeping. The sweets and savories are outstanding. Tea

Strolling along Fifth Avenue, you can visit Saks, Takashimaya, the St. Regis Hotel, The Peninsula Hotel, and Trump Tower.

sandwiches include a smoked salmon Napoleon, cucumber and watercress, curried-chicken salad with apple, a grilled cheese, lobster and shrimp salad on a Parmesan crisp, and *Labneh* (*kefir* cheese) on *Markouk* (Middle Eastern) bread. Scones are served with raspberry preserves and clotted cream. Sweets include vanilla and chocolate ganache cakes, a mocha éclair, carrot cake, fruit tarts, baklava, dates, strawberries and grapes. An all-vegan tea menu is available if you call ahead. Children enjoy the Teddy Bear Tea: peanut butter and jelly pinwheels, grilled cheese, and turkey and Swiss cheese sandwiches served with a soft-boiled egg and toast soldiers. Brownies, decorated cookies, and mini-cupcakes are the featured sweets.

• Afternoon tea served daily 2:30-5pm • Subway: F/Q/N/R/W trains to 57th St.; E/V trains to Fifth Ave.; 4/5/6 trains to 59th St. • Tel. 212-521-8155 • Reservations required • Child friendly • Major credit cards • www.daheshmuseum. • Full afternoon set tea. Children's menu. Vegan options. $$

Café SFA at Saks Fifth Avenue
611 Fifth Ave. btwn. 49th and 50th Sts.

The eighth-floor café offers a casual but comfortable venue for weary shoppers. Sit at one of the tables on the raised perimeter for excellent views of Rockefeller Center and St. Patrick's Cathedral. Afternoon tea is presented on a tiered server with cobalt-blue glass plates. Tea sandwiches include salmon, ham, and turkey on white bread. A miniature corn muffin, raisin scone, Devonshire cream and jams, butter cookies, and chocolates round out the treats. Mighty Leaf loose tea is served in a glass press pot with a perforated brewing basket. A lever in the lid allows you to halt the brewing when tea has reached desired strength.

• Afternoon tea Mon.-Fri. 3-5pm • Subway: E/V/6 trains to 51st Street/Lexington Ave.; B/D/F/V to 47th-50th Sts., Rockefeller Ctr. • Tel. 212-940-4080 • www.saks.com • Pot of tea. Full afternoon set tea. $$

Fitzers at the Fitzpatrick Manhattan Hotel
687 Lexington Ave. btwn. 56th & 57th Sts.

Warm-hearted Irish hospitality is offered in this unpretentious hotel owned and operated by the Fitzpatrick family. The restaurant serves traditional fare, including a full Irish breakfast, served all day, and two afternoon teas listed on the menu as low and high tea. The low tea consists of a choice of three sandwiches from a selection of six (ham, turkey, cucumber, cheese, tuna, and smoked salmon) or freshly baked scones
(continued on page 56)

"Guests are soothed with guitar melodies, and a glance at the ceiling, painted to resemble a blue sky dotted with pink-tinged clouds, promises a heavenly experience."

The Astor Court at the St. Regis Hotel
2 East 55th St. btwn. Madison and Fifth Aves.

John Jacob Astor, America's first multimillionaire, made a fortune in fur, tea and New York real estate. His great-grandson, Colonel John Jacob Astor IV, wanted to open a hotel where gentlemen and their families would feel as comfortable as guests in a luxurious private home. Designed by Trowbridge and Livingston, the 18-story building was, upon completion in 1904, the tallest building in what was then a residential area. Astor christened the establishment the St. Regis in honor of the French monk revered as the patron saint of hospitality.

The Astor Court is situated on a balustraded dais raised above the bustle of Fifth Avenue. Cream-colored marble is trimmed with 22 karat gold-leaf to project an elegant Beaux Arts atmosphere. Guests are soothed with guitar melodies, and a glance at the ceiling, painted to resemble a blue sky dotted with pink-tinged clouds, promises a heavenly experience.

Fifteen tables, crisply dressed in snowy Porthault linens, gather around an enormous bouquet of fresh flowers. Patrons are served on Limoges porcelain designed by Tiffany and Company exclusively for the hotel. A selection of 30 freshly-brewed loose teas and herbal tisanes are presented in sterling silver pots accompanied by individual strainers. The Astor Court Blend is a Harney & Sons custom mix of Earl Grey Supreme tea and ginger.

While the tea steeps, a three-tiered server, complete with fluted silver dome to keep the scones warm, is delivered to the table. Scones are served with Devonshire cream, homemade lemon curd, and seasonal jams. *New York Magazine* awarded the St. Regis four stars for "best sandwiches on the afternoon-tea circuit." The selection includes cucumber, smoked salmon, egg salad, shrimp salad, curried chicken, and goat cheese with sun-dried tomato served on a variety of breads. Assorted petits fours are varied enough to satisfy any sweet tooth. Champagne, port, and sherry are available for an additional price. Comfortably seated in plush chairs or perched on a plump banquette, guests are never rushed.

• Daily 2:30 and 4pm • Subway: E train to 5 Ave. at 53rd St., 4/5/6 trains to 51 St. • Tel. 212-753-4500 • Reservations recommended, but not required • www.stregis.com • Full afternoon set tea. Champagne. Port. Sherry. $$$

and preserves with assorted Irish cookies, served with a pot of tea. The high tea menu offers sandwiches, scones, and cookies. As is common in Ireland these days, the tea is Barry's brewed with a bag.

• Daily, including holidays, 3-6pm • Subway: 4/5/6/N/W/R/Q trains to 59th/Lexington • Tel. 212-784-2560 • Reservations recommended • Major credit cards • www.fitzpatrickhotel.com • Tea by the pot. Afternoon set tea. $

Fauchon
442 Park Ave. at 56th St.

Normandy native Auguste Fauchon began his career selling fruits and vegetables from a street cart. Success led to a small shop on the Place de la Madeleine around the corner from the Paris Opera. Women flocked to his elegant Grand Salon de Thé, built in 1898, to enjoy conversation over thé à la française.

Fauchon opened their flagship U.S. store on Park Avenue in August 2000. The chic pink and gold café offers a Parisian-style afternoon tea. Fauchon imports French flour, butter, mineral water, fleur de sel, and other ingredients to ensure the very best flavor and quality. Rich canapés and mini sandwiches include foie gras from Périgord, filet of Norwegian salmon, smoked salmon, egg salad, crabmeat, ham and cheese, and cucumber and watercress. A selection of petits fours, tea cakes, *moelleux* (almond-paste cookies) *macarons*, madeleines, and chocolates satisfy every sweet tooth. Salads, soups, omelettes, quiche, and other savories are also available.

French Tea Traditions

The Dutch East India Company introduced tea to France in 1636. There, as in Holland, doctors and philosophers debated the merits of the "drug" sold in apothecary shops. Some warned that tea consumption could damage delicate nervous systems, but Cardinal Mazarin believed it cured his gout. In 1680, Mm de Sevigne, a frequent visitor to court, wrote a letter to her daughter noting that one princess drank twelve cups of tea daily. This court correspondent was also the first European to record taking tea with milk.

Sevres produced exquisite porcelain tea wares for wealthy patrons who could afford to have artists paint portraits of them at their tea tables. Eventually, tea trickled down to the middle class, but the fashion really caught on in the 19th century when public tea salons opened in Paris. *Le five o'clock* was traditionally served with a variety of patisserie, rather than scones and finger sandwiches, and sometimes a cup of sinfully rich hot chocolate.

The shop sells its signature cakes, candies, and beautifully packaged confections as well as one hundred forty teas – original varieties and exclusive blends. There are classics from India, China, Sri Lanka, and Japan, as well tisanes, but the company is best known for its fruit-flavored teas, introduced in the 1960s, and flower-petal teas. The Fauchon Blend is a sophisticated mélange of orange, lemon, vanilla, and lavender. Unique products, such as black tea flavored with *capuacu*, an exotic Amazonian fruit, and mustard made with lapsang souchong, are introduced every year. Be sure to pick up a brochure that presents the tea collection arranged by Morning Teas, Meal Teas, All-Day Teas, Afternoon and Evening Teas.

- Afternoon tea Mon.-Fri. 11am-6pm
- Subway: 4/5/6 trains to 59th St.; N/R/W 5 Ave. at 59th St. • Tel. 212-308-5919
- Major Credit Cards • www.fauchon.com
- Tea by the pot. Afternoon set tea. A la carte menu. $$$

Franchia Tea House and Restaurant
12 Park Ave. btwn. 34th and 35th Sts.

South Korea grows green tea, and its traditions are descended from centuries-old ceremonies practiced in Buddhist monasteries. In the Korean tea ceremony called *Dado*, or *Tea Tao*, tea was drunk to help one harmonize with nature, detach from the busy world, and attain peace of mind.

William and Terri Choi, owners of Hangawi, an award-winning vegetarian restaurant, wanted to expand their philosophy of living a healthy life to include drinking tea. After studying in Korea, they opened their tea room named *Franchia*, Italian for lavish and generous.

The color palette of white (representing water's purity) and green (nature and tea) create a serene environment. Teas are brewed at the first floor tea bar; the second floor presents a more relaxed atmosphere. Workshops and private tea ceremonies are hosted in the third floor's traditional-style Korean tea room.

Franchia prides itself on a selection of wild green teas, valued for their strong *chi* (energy), hand-picked from rocky Korean mountain slopes. Tea is brewed gong-fu style and served in specially designed white china, the better to appreciate each tea's color. The teapot is kept warm on a

(continued on page 59)

"Afternoon tea
is served on the
Cocktail Terrace
overlooking the
majestic lobby
with its bas-
relief friezes and
the famous
Wheel-of-Life
mosaic-tiled
floor."

The Cocktail Terrace at the Waldorf-Astoria Hotel
301 Park Ave. btwn. 49th & 50th Sts.

In 1893, millionaire William Waldorf Astor launched the first Waldorf
Hotel. A cousin, Colonel John Jacob Astor, built the Astoria Hotel on
an adjacent site in 1897. In 1931 the joined Waldorf-Astoria opened
its doors. An official landmark building, the Art Deco property
occupies an entire city block on New York's Park Avenue.

The Waldorf-Astoria is synonymous with elegance and grandeur.
Celebrities, diplomats, and other fashionable folks are often spotted
in the lobby. Afternoon tea is served on the Cocktail Terrace
overlooking the majestic lobby with its bas-relief friezes, mahogany
paneling, marble columns, and the famous Wheel-of-Life mosaic-tiled
floor.

A variety of loose leaf teas – lapsang souchong, Formosa oolong,
Darjeeling, Dragon Pearl, and jasmine – are served by the pot. Finger
sandwiches feature traditional fillings – smoked salmon on pumpernickel, turkey, ham and brie, egg salad, cream cheese and cucumber.
Delicious orange-currant-buttermilk scones served with Devonshire
cream and preserves, almond pound cake, a raspberry custard tart,
and other pastries round out the tea treats.

In conjunction with the Alexander Doll Company, the hotel launched a
popular Saturday afternoon Tea for Tots. The three-course snack
consists of caffeine-free loose-leaf teas chosen by a panel of young
taste-testers, accompanied by peanut butter and jelly, ham and
cheese, and tuna salad finger sandwiches with assorted strawberry,
vanilla, and chocolate crème pastries.

Master Tea Blender John Harney often presents a lively tea-lore and
etiquette lesson. After tea, pianist-singer Daryl Sherman gathers
children around Cole Porter's Steinway Grand piano for a chorus of
"I'm A Little Teapot" and other classics. Youngsters go home with a
certificate of participation and a goodie bag filled with teas, sweets,
and literature. One lucky child wins a Madame Alexander® Doll.

• Closed during July and August. Open: Wed.-Sun. 3-5:30pm, Tea for
Tots: Sat. 2:30-5pm • Subway: 6 train to 51st St. and Lexington
Ave., V to 53rd and Lexington, B/D/F/V trains to Rockefeller Center •
Tel. 212-872-4818 • Reservations required • Child friendly • Dress
code: Smart casual – jeans not permitted • Major credit cards
• www.waldorfastoria.com • Tea by the pot. Afternoon set tea.
Children's menu. $$$

candle-heated ceramic ring and served with a strainer and hot water carafe. Vietnamese green teas, floral-green tea blends, oolongs, black tea, herbal infusions, freshly squeezed fruit-tea smoothies, iced tea, and bubble tea are also available. A chai latte made with Darjeeling tea and soy milk is a sweet treat for vegans.

Franchia's menu is strictly vegetarian, and the cooking is a delicious blend of Korean, Asian, and Western cuisines. The prix fixe Royal Tea Tray presents two different pots of tea plus tasting portions of appetizers such as vegetable dumplings, green-tea-zucchini or tofu-scallion pancakes, sushi, mini patties, and spring rolls with dipping sauces. Sweets include green tea bread, rice cookies, *mocci* (rice-ball cake), soy cheesecake and *yak gwa* (cookies), and red or white bean jellies. Franchia teas and meals are available for take-out. A small first-floor shop sells green tea, tea accessories, and their signature china serveware.

A number of New York tea rooms, such as Franchia, offer menus to please vegetarians and vegans.

• Mon.-Sat. 11:30am-10pm. Sun. noon-10pm • Subway: 6 train to 33rd St., Park Ave. • Tel. 212-213-1001 • Reservations required • www.franchia.com • Major credit cards • Tea by the pot. Vegetarian afternoon set tea. A la carte menu. $

Goodmans at Bergdorf Goodman
754 Fifth Ave. btwn. 58th and 69th Sts.

Goodmans, located on the lower level of the women's store, is a narrow room crisply furnished with small square tables and striped banquettes. Fresh flowers add a spark of color. A plate of tea sandwiches – cucumber, chicken and watercress, gravlax – and assorted sweets are available with a choice of ten bagged teas from Harney & Sons.

The Vintage Tea Shop is located on Bergdorf's seventh floor, home to a rich array of tableware, linens, and decorative accessories. The antique, vintage, and retro ceramic tea things are displayed in color groups, making it simple to add to your own collections. Shop here for hard-to-find tea textiles: embroidered tea cosies, starched napkins, towels, and table linens. Silver cutlery, tea services, toast racks, and toasting forks are offered, and every item in the shop is in perfect condition. Mariage Frères teas and candles, Reva Paul decorated sugars and

tea-flavored chocolates are sold on the same floor.

• Subway: N/R/E/V at 5th Ave.; F/N/R/W/4/5/6 to 59th Street/Lexington Ave. • Tel. 212-753-7300 • Afternoon tea Mon.-Sat. 2:30-6pm • Major credit cards • Afternoon set tea. $

Istana at the New York Palace Hotel
455 Madison Ave. btwn. 50th and 51st Sts.

Istana restaurant once flirted with a *tapas* tea, but now it no longer serves afternoon tea. However, it is possible to order a pot of hot tea or four uniquely named and blended iced tea drinks. The Palace Coup, a fully caffeinated mixture of raspberry, vanilla, peach, mango and green tea, is described as the "ultimate power surge." The Hangover, a blend of fresh ginger, mint and green tea "provides the kick needed on those less than chipper mornings." The Serene helps you collect your thoughts with a peaceful decaf mix of chamomile and peppermint. The Comforter is a cinnamon, apple and green tea concoction with a scent to "bring back childhood memories."

• Daily 6:30am-11:30pm • Subway: 6 train to 51st St. • Tel. 212-888-7000 • Major credit cards • Tea by the pot or glass. $

The Lobby Lounge at the Four Seasons Hotel
57 E. 57th St. btwn. Madison and Park Aves.

I. M. Pei, the Chinese-born modernist architect, designed a stunning limestone tower for the Four Seasons hotel. The award-winning lofty lobby soars from marble floor to onyx ceiling, creating one of the city's most dramatic locations.

Afternoon tea features turkey and Brie on sourdough bread, smoked salmon on pumpernickel, deviled ham salad on seven-grain bread, grilled vegetables in a sun-dried tomato wrap, and scones with strawberry jam and Devonshire cream. For a sweet finish there's raspberry financier, a coffee cream puff, a strawberry tart, banana bread, and a piece of densely-layered Opera cake. The selection of loose-leaf tea includes three greens, a traditional oolong as well as one blended with Darjeeling, eight blacks, one of which is a hand-smoked Alderwood Yunnan tea, and an "Italian festive tea swirled with a hint of vanilla and the zest of lemons and oranges, called *Pannetone."* Apple rooibos, scented with mango, marigold petals, and whole rosebuds, is the hotel's signature blend. There are five other herbal infusions. The menu thoughtfully provides a key to indicate which teas are best taken with milk, sugar, honey or lemon.

SUBMITTED PHOTO

• Daily 3-5pm • Subway: N/R/W/4/5/6 trains to 59th St. • Tel. 212-758-5700 • Reservations required for parties of five or more. • www.fourseasons.com • Major credit cards • Afternoon set tea. Champagne. Wine. $$$

The Rotunda at the Pierre Hotel
2 E. 61st St. at Fifth Ave.

As suits a grande dame, the Rotunda is richly ornate. Elaborate floor-to-ceiling murals are tucked between faux-marble Greco-Roman columns, depicting socialites frolicking with satyrs and nymphs. Fluffy clouds flit across the blue-domed ceiling and two tiers of gilt sconces shed a soft glow on the lush floral arrangement. Tables laid with damask-patterned linens and flowered Ginori porcelain are ranged around the room.

Formally presented on a three-tired server, tea sandwiches change seasonally but typically include egg salad, a smoked-salmon Napoleon, a chicken salad with chives wrap, and a cucumber sandwich. Scones are served with Devonshire cream and preserves – peach and Little Scarlet made with *Fraises des Bois* strawberries. Assorted teacakes – vanilla and chocolate éclairs, shortbread, a vanilla madeleine, a raspberry fruit tart, and fruit cake – complete the tea treats. Tea selections by Harney & Sons include Royal Rotunda, a blend of black teas, supreme vanilla, black currant, and Earl Grey created especially for the Pierre. A dozen other blacks, a green tea, and herbal infusions are also available, but whatever you choose, you'll have to wait for the waiter to refill your cup.

• Daily 3-5:30pm • Subway: N/R/W trains to 60th St. • Tel. 212-940-8195 • www.fourseasons.com/pierre • Reservations not accepted • Afternoon set tea. A la carte menu. Champagne. $$$

"Elegantly served on a footed lacquered tray, this generous assortment is one of the city's most delicious and reasonably priced teas."

The Tea Box at Takashimaya
693 Fifth Ave. btwn. 54th and 55th Sts.

The Tea Box is located on the lower level of Takashimaya. The parent company is one of Japan's oldest (1831) and largest retailers dedicated to providing unique items to discerning customers. An eclectic assortment of tableware and textiles is housed on the third floor. Another shop, adjacent to the Tea Box restaurant, sells an enormous variety of beautifully packaged loose teas, teapots, and accessories including cherry-wood tea scoops, whisks, timers, trays, and bamboo charcoal to sweeten brewing water.

After a frenzied shopping spree, the muted tones of the Tea Box's two tiny dining rooms will restore serenity. Forty types of loose tea and tisanes are available; a rose-petal Chinese black tea is the signature blend. The afternoon tea menu offers three open-faced finger sandwiches – salmon or cucumber on pressed rice, chicken with *wasabi* (horseradish) mayonnaise on Japanese bread, and a vegetarian or crab rice-paper roll. Sweet or savory samplers feature three butter or vegetable cookies. French pastries and mousses include a creamy panna cotta, baked chocolate-orange pudding with orange shortbread, a chocolate truffle, apple spring rolls and a black-rice pudding with coconut, whipped cream, and seasonal fruit. There's even an Earl Grey tea ice cream with green tea shortbread. Elegantly served on a footed lacquered tray, this generous assortment is one of the city's most delicious and reasonably priced teas.

• Closed Sundays except Sept.-Dec. Open: Mon.-Sat. 10am-6pm, Thurs. till 8pm • Subway: E train to 5th Ave./53rd St., 6 train to 51st St. • Tel. 212-350-0100 • Afternoon set tea. Snacks. Tea by the pot. $

Shopping Sites for Tea Lovers

Adriana's Caravan
87 E 42nd St., Grand Central Terminal

Conveniently located in Grand Central Terminal's fabulous Food Hall, Adriana's sells "every ingredient for every recipe you've ever read," as well as loose and bagged tea from Harney and Sons, Kusmi, Tea Forte, and Taylors of Harrogate. Colorful teapots, brewing accessories, and custom tea-themed gift baskets are available.
• Mon.-Fri. 7am-9pm, Sat. 10am-7pm, Sun. 11am-6pm • Subway: 4/5/6/7/S trains to Grand Central • Tel. 212-972-8804 • Major credit cards • www.adrianascaravan.com

Bernardaud
499 Park Ave. btwn. 56th and 57th Sts.

Bernardaud is one of France's oldest porcelain producers, tracing its origin to 1863. The flagship American store displays a fine array of dinnerware including teapots in formal designs as well as contemporary classics. At the back of the shop is a counter where you may sip the tea of the day in the china cup of your choice. Bernardaud sells tea attractively packaged in tins striped to match their *Galerie Royale* porcelain pattern. Fourteen types of loose tea – caramel, citrus, Damas, jasmine Chung Hao, lapsang souchong – are available as well as a French-style hot chocolate and assorted chocolates and nuts.
• Closed weekends August through Labor Day. Open Mon.-Sat. 10am-6pm, Thurs. till 7pm • Subway: 4/5/6/N/R trains to 59th St. • Tel. 212-371-4300 • Major credit cards • www.bernardaud.fr

Fortunoff
681 Fifth Ave. btwn. 53rd and 54th Sts.

Breeze past the bling-bling on the first floor and take the elevator to the fourth floor where more than two hundred china patterns and antique silver tea sets, trays, and cutlery are looking for a new home.
• Mon.-Sat. 10am-6pm. Thurs. till 7pm
• Subway: E/V trains to 5th Ave. at 53rd St. • Tel. 212-758-6660

James Robinson
480 Park Ave. at 58th St.

Established in 1912, James Robinson is still operated by the same family of passionate collectors. It serves as one of Manhattan's premier sources for antique English and European tableware. Mahogany cases hold porcelain and silver pieces, but the knowledgeable staff will take that Georgian Worchester tea set out of the case for you to examine the hand-painted, gilded

raspberry design. The back room houses a museum with rare finds such as a George III traveling tea set – three sterling silver caddies, twelve tea spoons, a mote spoon and pair of sugar nippers, fitted in their original leather carrying case. Hand-hammered silver replicas of antique tableware may be custom ordered.

• Mon.-Sat. 10am-5pm • Subway: E/N/R/V/W trains to 5th Ave. • Tel. 212-752-6166 • Major credit cards

Katagiri
224-226 E. 59th St. btwn. 2nd & 3rd. Aves.

The immigrant Katagiri brothers opened their original store in 1907. Shop here for authentic Japanese groceries, tea, and serveware.

• Grocery store daily 10am-8pm, gift shop 10am-7pm • Subway: 4/5/6/F/N/R/W trains to 59th St. Lexington Ave. • Tel. 212-755-3566 • www.katagiri.com • Major credit cards

Oren's Daily Roast
87 E 42nd St; Lexington Ave. at 43rd St. (Grand Central Terminal Market)

In addition to coffee, Oren's has loose and bagged teas at multiple locations throughout the city. The shops also carry cast-iron, glass, and ceramic teapots, colorful mugs and brewing accessories.

• www.orensdailyroast.com • Tel. 212-953-1028

Pierre Marcolini Chocolatier
485 Park Ave. btwn. 56th and 57th Sts.

Visit here for tea and tea-infused chocolates crafted by world champion pastry chef and chocolatier Pierre Marcolini. He sells thirteen loose teas with exotic names and ingredients – Cinnamon Star, a blend of lemon, cinnamon, ginger, cardamom, pepper, and vanilla – as well as a First-Flush Assam and Second-Flush Darjeelings. There are three rooibos blends. All tea selections were developed in collaboration with Vincent Perpete of Salon de thè Comptoir Florian in Brussels.

• Mon.-Sat. 8am-7pm. Sun. noon-5pm
• Subway: 4/5/6/N/R trains to 59th St.
• Tel. 212-755-5150 • Major credit cards
• www.marcolinichocolatier.com

Secrets of the Leaf
The South African herb rooibos comes from the leaves of the Aspalathus linoaris, *not from* Camellia sinensis; *it is naturally caffeine-free.*

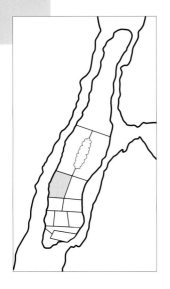

Midtown West

If you love fine art, good food, theater, and Rockefeller Center, Midtown West is the place to be. Tea venues in this part of the city are glamorous and memorable.

Gotham Lounge at the Peninsula Hotel
700 Fifth Ave. at 55th St.; enter on W. 55th

Many Beaux Arts architectural details remain in this 1905 building, providing a blend of modern accents and old-world elegance. The Gotham Lounge and bar is a favorite with the business crowd. The subdued space is crisply tailored with tan, black, and camel-colored upholstery. Floor-to-ceiling arched windows overlook the busy street and provide a dramatic backdrop for tea.

The floor-to-ceiling arched windows in the Gotham Lounge overlook the busy street and provide a dramatic backdrop for tea.

The afternoon tea menu presents sophisticated sandwiches – smoked salmon on brioche with crème fraiche and caviar, egg salad with cream cheese and cucumber, roast beef, Boursin cream, horseradish and asparagus salad on whole wheat, herb-roasted shrimp with roasted-tomato hummus, and a smoked turkey wrap with cranberry aioli. Scones are accompanied by Devonshire cream and fruit preserves. Sweets include lemon poppy-seed, banana-walnut, and chocolate macadamia tea breads with mini fruit tarts and assorted chocolate pastries.

Five loose leaf teas are blended in Hong Kong exclusively for the hotel. Taylors of Harrogate supplies eight others including a green-chamomile-lemon grass iced tea. A glass of Louis Roederer Brut champagne turns a Peninsula afternoon tea into a royal experience.

• Daily 2:30-5pm • Subway: E train to 5th Ave. at 53rd St. • Tel. 212-247-2200 • Reservations recommended • Major credit cards • Tea by the pot. Afternoon set tea. Champagne. $$$

Kinokuniya Bookstore Café
10 West 49th St. btwn. 5th and 6th Aves.

Kinokuniya sells Japanese language books and magazines, as well as English books about the Japanese tea ceremony, ceramics, and teahouses. Selecting an addition to your tea library is thirsty work. Take a break at the café bar for a sandwich or piece of cake (green tea tiramisu, chocolate soufflé, or chestnut cream) with a pot of freshly brewed Assam, Earl Grey, Golden Kenya, or Matcha tea. They also sell Ito En packaged teas. On Friday afternoons, the café serves *wagashi* (sweets) made with *azuki* bean paste, rice flour, sugar, and green tea. Prices include tax and tips.

• Daily 11am-7pm • Subway: B/D/F/Q trains at 47-50 Sts., Rockefeller Center
• Tel. 212-765-7766 • Major credit cards
• Tea by the pot. Snacks. Sweets. $

La Maison du Chocolat
30 Rockefeller Center btwn. 5th & 6th Aves.

Additional location Upper East Side. See flagship listing on page 76.

• Subway: B/D/F/V to 47th-50th St. at Rockefeller Center • Tel. 212-265-9404
• www.lamaisonduchocolat.com • Tea by the pot. Pastries and chocolates. $

The Star Lounge at the Ritz-Carlton Hotel, Central Park
50 Central Park South btwn. 5th & 6th Aves.

The hotel has the ambience of an elegant townhouse, but the Star Lounge, tucked between the reception area and the bar, can get noisy. Arrange to sit with your back to the front desk, facing the harpist. The space is warm and welcoming with burled-wood walls, antique crystal chandeliers, and high-backed chairs and sofas upholstered in pale colors. Porcelain tea lights twinkle on individual tables.

SUBMITTED PHOTO

Afternoon tea is served in stages on a silver tiered stand. There are delicious, bite-sized sandwiches: cucumber on brioche with dill-cream cheese, smoked salmon with caper salad, egg salad with tomato, prosciutto with mascarpone cheese, and a lemony crab-filled éclair on a chive baton. Scrumptious sugar-crusted scones are served with clotted cream and raspberry, pineapple, and blood-orange preserves supplied by Sarabeth's. The third course – assorted petits fours – arrives on a two-tiered silver server.

Nine types of black tea, three greens, and three herbal infusions are offered. Spring Blend is a "hypnotic" mix of white and green tea combined with spring flowers. The house blend is a whole-fruit mix of wild strawberries, blackberries, and raspberries called Nobo. Loose leaves are brewed by the pot and poured by the waitress. While you're waiting for a refill, search for the leopard hidden in the exotic blossoms on your Persia-patterned Wedgwood china plate.

• Daily 2:30-5:30pm • Subway: F train to 57th St. • Tel. 212- 308-9100 • Reservations required • Major credit cards • Afternoon set tea. Champagne. Wine. $$$

Salontea at the City Club Hotel
55 W. 44th St. btwn. 5th and 6th Aves.

As early as the 17th century, elegant women hosted salons where artists, aristocrats, and intellectuals gathered to amuse themselves over a cup of tea. Soignée Tracy Stern presides over a contemporary Salontea, inspired by her encounter with European tea rooms while studying art-history abroad.

The tea room on the second-floor mezzanine seats twelve in high-backed, upholstered chairs drawn around tables draped in saffron-colored voile. Flickering votive candles beam the gleam of the glass teapot perched on its silvery platform. Tracy named each of her estate tea blends after a character one might have met during the golden age of the salon. Society Hostess is a naturally decaffeinated, vanilla-infused china black tea. The Artist is a Ceylon from the Kenilworth Estate. Fashionable Dandy is China black tea scented with bergamot oil. The Writer is an Indian chai spiced with cinnamon, cloves, and cardamom. The Musician is an herbal Rooibos blended with hibiscus and rose. The Romantic is Chur She green tea blended with jasmine flowers.

Michelin-rated chef Daniel Boulud, owner of the hotel's DB Bistro Moderne restaurant, prepares treats that arrive on a tiered silver caddy garnished with rose petals. You'll enjoy heart-shaped scones served with Double Devonshire cream and quince-rose petal jelly, tea sandwiches including one made with goat cheese, black truffles, pecans and olives, designer canapés, and decadent desserts including chocolates flown in from Parisian patisserie, Ladurée. Tracy considers the space to be an extension of her home, and it shows.

• Closed Memorial Day to Labor Day. Otherwise open Tues.-Sat. 3-5pm • Subway: N/Q/R/S/W/1/2/3/7 trains to Times Square, 4/5/6/7 trains to Grand Central Station at 42nd St. • Tel. 212-398-1323 • Reservations required • Major credit cards • www.salonteas.com • Afternoon set tea. $$$

Terrace 5 at the Museum of Modern Art
9 W. 53rd St. btwn. Fifth and Sixth Aves.

In 1929, Abby Aldrich Rockefeller and two friends opened a small museum to house a small collection of modern art - Cézanne, Gauguin, Seurat and van Gogh. Over time, the museum expanded to include film, photography, industrial design, and printed books. Today, the permanent collection boasts some of the best known examples of European modernist art and avant-garde American abstract expressionism.

Located in the renovated and expanded Museum of Modern Art, the Terrace 5 café is a jewel box with a spectacular fifth-floor view of the Sculpture Garden. Black cast iron teapots and fresh flowers provide strong contrast to the white décor and Danish furniture from leading modernist designers. Loose leaf teas, from Vancouver's T company, are steeped to order in two-cup pots. The MOMA signature blend adds a touch of Lapsang Souchong to Chinese black.

Terrace 5 is a full-service chocolate and dessert restaurant where guests may also indulge in savory bites. Leading artisanal chocolatiers such as Chocolat Moderne and Maison du Chocolate supply chocolates and delectable ice cream coupes, cakes, and tarts. There's a creamy chai latte as well as hot chocolate with homemade marshmallows. Savories such as Catsmo smoked salmon with cucumber, crème fraiche, and trout caviar, or shrimp and vegetable spring rolls are delicious stand-ins for traditional tea sandwiches.

• Open only to museum visitors. Closed Tuesday. Otherwise open 11am-5 pm. Open till 7:30pm on Fri. • Subway: E/V trains to 5th Ave. at 53rd St.; B/D/F trains to 47-50 Sts. • Rockefeller Center • Tel. 212-333-1288 • Major credit cards • www.moma.org • Pot of tea. Savories. Sweets. $$

Shopping Sites for Tea Lovers

Jean's Silversmiths
16 W. 45th St. btwn. 5th and 6th Aves.

Established in 1910, Jean's Silversmiths is a narrow shop crammed with estate, vintage and retro silver including antique tea sets, trays, pitchers, cutlery, candlesticks

and napkin rings. The shop can help locate and match missing set pieces. Jean's restores damaged silver and provides polishing and engraving.
• Mon.-Fri. 9am-4:45pm • Subway: S/4/5/6/7 trains to Grand Central 42nd St. • Tel. 212-575-0723 • Major credit cards • www.jeanssilversmiths.com

MacKenzie-Childs
14 West 57th St.

Fanciful handcrafted ceramics, enamelware, and decorative accessories comprise MacKenzie-Childs home collection based on tradition with a twist. You'll find colorful tea kettles decorated with faux cinnabar, bone or stone-bead finials, teapots, mugs

and cups decorated with courtly checks, stripes and cabbage roses, as well as beribboned, tea-themed Christmas ornaments.
• Mon.-Wed. 10am-6pm, Thurs.-Sat. 10am-7pm, Sun. noon-5pm • Subway: N/Q/R/W trains to 57th St. at 7th Ave. • Tel. 212-570-6050 • www.mackenzie-childs.com • Major credit cards

Minamoto Kitchoan
608 Fifth Ave.; W. 49th St. btwn. 5th and 6th Aves.

Minamoto Kitchoan, the New York branch of a famous Japanese confectionary shop, is right around the corner from Kinokuniya. Shop for wagashi cunningly crafted to represent seasonal fruits as well as flowers and ginko leaves. The shop also sells packaged loose tea and bottles of chilled green tea to-go.
• Sun.-Thurs. 10am-7:30pm. Fri.-Sat. 10am-8pm • Subway: B/D/F/Q trains at 47-50 Sts., Rockefeller Center • Tel. 212-489-3747 • www.kitchoan.com • Major credit cards

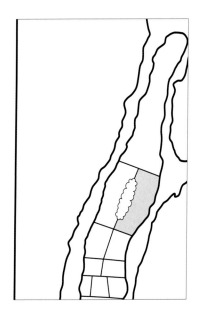

Upper East Side

The Upper East Side boasts some of the city's most exclusive residences, from penthouses with Central Park views to Gracie Mansion, an 18th-century country house now home to the mayor. Fifth Avenue is world famous for luxury shopping, but many of the city's best-loved museums, including the Metropolitan Museum of Art and the Guggenheim Museum, are located here. Tea lovers may enjoy elegantly formal afternoon teas, contemporary Asian-fusion teas, and artful museum meals.

Alice's Tea Cup Chapter II

156 E. 64th St. btwn. Lexington and Third Aves.

Sisters Haley and Lauren Fox, lifelong tea lovers, created two cozy-casual tea parlors at which everyone seems to feel welcome. Proud grandparents snap photos of a baby sleeping in his father's arms while mom beams her approval. A bearded young man flirts with a pretty girl whose hair is colored magenta to match her glasses. Guests, seated at mismatched wooden tables or lounging on banquettes, may choose from 120 types of loose tea. Tea is brewed in double-filtered water and served in a china pot equipped with a decorative drip-catcher. Four scrumptious set teas, including one just for children, are available and portions are generous. See main listing page 90.

At Alice's Tea Cup Chapter II, four scrumptious set teas, including one just for children, are available. Portions are generous.

• Closed Mondays. Hours: Tues.-Fri. 8am-11pm, Thurs. and Sat. 10am-midnight, Sun. 8am-8pm. Afternoon tea served any time • Subway: 4/5/6 trains to 59th St.; F train to 63rd St. at Lexington Ave. • Tel. 212-486-9200 • Reservations required for parties of six or more. • Child friendly • Major credit cards • www.alicesteacup.com • Tea by the pot. Afternoon set tea. Children's menu. A la carte menu. $$

Café Sabarsky at the Neue Galerie Museum

1048 Fifth Avenue at 86th St.

Art dealer and museum organizer Serge Sabarsky shared a passion for early 20th-century German-Austrian art with business-man and art collector Ronald S. Lauder. They dreamed of opening a museum, and after Sabarsky died, Lauder created the Neue Galerie in tribute to his friend. The building housing the museum was completed in 1914 by Carrere and Hastings, architects of the New York Public Library. Once home to Mrs. Cornelius Vanderbilt III, it was inaugurated as a museum in 2001. The second floor gallery explores the relationship between the fine arts – Gustav Klimt, Egon Schiele – and the decorative arts created at the Wiener Werkstatte. Even though you can't take the

beautiful teapots home, you may enjoy tea and a torte in the café.

The décor is straight out of *fin-de-siecle* Vienna with Hoffman sconces, marble-topped tables, bentwood chairs, and dark wood paneling. The Austrian theme continues with Viennese pastries – *Dobosch* torte dense with mocha buttercream, *Klimttorte*, a hazelnut cake with bitter chocolate, *Linzer* torte, *Sacher* torte, strawberry jelly roll, jelly doughnuts, and a flaky apple strudel *mit schlag* (heavy whipped cream). For heartier appetites, the menu offers soup, salads, savory entrees, and a variety of open-face sandwiches.

To drink, there's unsweetened hot chocolate served in a bowl accompanied by whipped cream, a miniature whisk, and a glass of water to rinse your whisk or cleanse your palate. New York's own Serendipitea supplies a chocolate-flavored tea with vanilla notes, a delicious pineapple-papaya blend, blood orange, chamomile-lavender, as well as Ceylon and several other standards. If you still hanker for a Viennese-style teapot, visit the Design Shop, which sells exquisitely crafted reproductions.

The second floor gallery at the Neue Galerie Museum explores the relationship between the fine arts – Gustav Klimt, Egon Schiele – and the decorative arts created at the Wiener Werkstatte.

• Closed Tuesdays. Hours: Mon. and Wed. 9am-6pm, Thur.-Sun. 9am-9pm • Subway: 4/5/6 trains to 86th St. • Tel. 212-288-0665 • www.neuegalerie.org • Major credit cards • Tea by the pot and pastries. Retail shop. $

SUBMITTED PHOTO

The Gallery at the Carlyle Hotel
35 E. 76th St. at Madison Ave.

This exotic tea parlor, inspired by a room in Istanbul's Topkapi Palace, features hand-painted wallpaper with vignettes of Turkish treasures. Two levels seat guests on upholstered red-velvet chairs or carpet-covered divans. Afternoon tea includes a pot of loose tea, finger sandwiches (ham, egg salad,

(continued on page 75)

The Hotel Plaza Athénée

37 E. 64th St. btwn. Park and Madison Aves.

The Plaza Athénée is the only hotel in the United States to offer *Thieme's Echte Thee*. Developed in the Netherlands by Tea Master Karel Christiaan, the teas are brewed with soft *Fiji* water chosen for its low mineral content. Mr. Christiaan trained the staff on the fine points of brewing in a teapot that utilizes reverse osmosis to prevent the leaves from over-steeping.

The tea card lists fourteen varieties ranging from traditional blends to specialties such as Anti-Jet-Lag herbal infusion. The Plaza Athénée Blend is a combination of First and Second-Flush Darjeelings, Chinese Keemun, jasmine, supreme rose, and Earl Grey. Afternoon tea treats include sandwiches (salmon cucumber-cream cheese, herbed shrimp salad, prosciutto wrapped in a baguette), large raisin scones dusted with powdered sugar, a chocolate brownie, chocolate-dipped strawberries, fruit tarts, apple pie, and lemon curd with a cherry coulis.

A full afternoon tea may be enjoyed in the romantic Bar Seine lounge, decorated with red-lacquered walls, leather floors, and scorched rattan chairs, or in the Euro-Asian ambience of the Arabelle restaurant.

• Daily 2:30-5pm • Subway: 4/5/6 trains to 59th St.; F train to 63rd St. at Lexington Ave. • Tel. 212-734-9100 • Reservations recommended for groups of seven or more • Major credit cards • www.plaza-athenee.com • Afternoon set tea. Champagne. $$$

chicken breast, cucumber, and a cream cheese-raisin bread roulade), an enormous toasted raisin scone or crumpets served with Devonshire cream and preserves, and miniature pastries – raspberry and passion fruit tarts, coffee éclair, and a slice of chocolate Opera cake.

Ludwig Bemelmans, the free-spirited author and artist of the beloved *Madeline* books, bartered accommodations for himself in exchange for painting the hotel bar's murals. Perhaps that rakish rabbit, posing in polka-dot pants, is drinking an Earl Grey *MarTEAni*. The specialty cocktail, infused with Earl Grey tea, lemon juice, simple syrup, and egg whites, is sure to add to your delight as you inspect the whimsical illustrations. The Madeline Experience offers a special children's menu, storytelling, and piano music.

The gift shop at the Asia Society and Museum stocks a fabulous collection of fashion accessories, jewelry, tea books, traditional and contemporary teapots, brewing accessories, and Serendipitea loose tea.

• Daily 3-5:30pm. Children's tea Wed.-Sun., noon-4pm • Subway: 6 train to 77th St. • Tel. 212-744-1600 • Child friendly • Major credit cards • www.thecarlyle.com • Tea by the pot. Afternoon set tea. Children's menu. Champagne. Tea-infused cocktails. $$$

The Garden Court Café at the Asia Society and Museum
725 Park Ave. at E. 70th St.

The Asia Society, founded in 1956 by John D. Rockefeller III, is an international organization dedicated to deepening understanding between the people of Asia and the United States. Masterpieces from the Rockefeller Collection are on display year round, and the Society sponsors arts events, seminars, and publications. The gift shop stocks a fabulous collection of fashion accessories, jewelry, tea books, traditional and contemporary teapots, brewing accessories, and Serendipitea loose tea.

The Garden Court Café, operated by Great Performances, is located off the lobby. Weeping Podocarpus trees, flowering vines, and suspended sculptures crafted by contemporary Asian artists warm the glass-enclosed space. Spacious and flooded with light, this is one of the city's most serene locations for tea.

Nine long-leaf loose teas and two herbals are offered including a Green Sea Anemone, an organic Darjeeling, and *Siam*, a black tea blended with mint, clove, cardamom, and cinnamon. Salads, vegetarian sushi and spring rolls, noodle dishes, soups, and a traditional chicken *Tikka* sandwich served on *nan* bread are some of the savories. For an afternoon tea, order the Bento Lunch Box sampler or an exotic dessert. The Trio of

Brulees – Tahitian vanilla, chocolate, and pumpkin - is tempting. But so is the Baby Banana Tempura served with green tea ice cream and sake sauce.

• Closed Mondays. Hours: Tues-Sun 11am-3pm for lunch, 3-4:30pm for desserts and beverages, Fri. 11am-9pm full menu. Call for summer hours. • Subway: 4/5 trains to 68th St. and Lexington Ave. • Tel. 212-570-5202 • Reservations not required • www.asiasociety.org • Major credit cards • Tea by the pot. A la carte menu. $$

Kings' Carriage House
251 E. 82nd St. at Second Ave.

Elizabeth King and her Irish husband, Paul Farrell, converted a bookshop into a quaint tea room. The two-story brick carriage house is decorated to resemble an Irish manor house, complete with stuffed stag heads and hunting prints. Afternoon tea is enjoyed in the Willow Room overlooking a wee garden. The set tea provides cucumber and salmon sandwiches, savory tartlets, scones with cream and jam, and assorted sweets. There is no a la carte tea menu, but children enjoy their own selections: cucumber triangles, cream cheese-jelly rounds, cinnamon toast hearts, cheese-pickle triangle, banana-strawberry-marshmallow tarts, scones, cream and jam, fresh berries, fairy cakes, shortbread cookies, and gingerbread served with a pot of raspberry tea. Bridal showers and other special event teas may be booked in a private room.

• Daily 3-5pm • Subway: 4/5/6 trains to 86th St. Lexington Ave. • Tel. 212-734-5490 • Reservations required • Child friendly • Major credit cards • Tea by the pot. Afternoon set tea. $$

La Maison du Chocolat
1018 Madison Ave. btwn. 77th & 78th Sts.

The main business of this Paris-based chocolatier is exquisite hand-made confections such as truffle-robed chocolates infused with champagne-cognac, chocolate-covered fruits and nuts, and rich chocolate pastries. This small, elegant tea salon allows chocoholics to indulge in a pot of hot tea (five choices) with delectable desserts. Three-times a year, *Parcours Initiatique* tasting sessions explore the subtle associations between coffee, chocolates, and tea. To inquire about available dates and prices, phone 212-265-9404. Second location Midtown West; see listing page 65.

• Mon.-Sat. 10am-7pm, Sun. noon- 6:30pm • Subway: 6 train to 77th St. • Tel. 212-744-7117 • www.lamaisonduchocolat.com • Major credit cards • Tea by the pot. Pastries and chocolates. $

The two-story Kings' Carriage House is decorated to resemble an Irish manor house, complete with stuffed stag heads and hunting prints.

SUBMITTED PHOTO

"This serene space is as spare as a haiku poem."

Kai Restaurant above Ito En

822 Madison Ave. btwn. 68th and 69th Sts.

In 1966, two brothers started Ito En, now the world's largest green tea supplier. They targeted young, on-the-go Japanese as the ideal market for bottled tea. This flagship American store is a temple to tea, spare but elegant, with cherry-wood fixtures and floral arrangements. The store employs a professional tea taster and stocks 75 fine teas. There are unique greens such as a rustic mixture of leaves and stems, five types of powdered green matcha, and eleven kinds of sencha. They also carry Chinese greens, whites, blacks, and oolongs. Highly perishable teas are refrigerated at forty degrees; samples are displayed in glass bottles with long noses so that you can sniff the leaves. Tea specialist Kai Anderson conducts brewing classes and advises on tea-food pairings. There's also an exquisite assortment of teapots, from Yixing to Wedgwood, brewing accessories, and beautiful boxed gift sets.

Kai ("gathering place") Restaurant is located above the shop. The name also refers to multi-course *kaiseki* snacks served five hundred years ago in Zen Buddhist temples to accompany the tea ceremony. This serene space is as spare as a haiku poem. Chef Yorinobu Yamasaki prepares the elegant fare in a variety of shapes, colors, and textures to celebrate the seasons. The menu changes monthly but always consists of a pot of one of Ito En's artisanal teas served with sweets and savories such as tiny tea sandwiches, miniature green tea scones, tea-flavored rice balls, quiche, chocolate-covered almonds dusted with matcha powder, and addictive Earl Grey-flavored candied grapefruit peels. You may also choose from the a la carte dessert menu.

Filtered water is used for brewing teas – six Japanese greens including an exotic *sakura* (cherry blossom) sencha, six blacks (four Chinese, one each from India and Sri Lanka), a delicate White Peony, as well as tisanes and flower teas. Four flavors of Ito En's signature unsweetened, bottled teas are also available.

• Ito En is open Mon.-Sat. 10am-8pm, Sun. noon-5pm. Kai Restaurant is open daily noon-4pm • Subway: 6 train to 68th St. at Hunter College • Reservations required • Tel. 212-988-7111 • Major credit cards • www.itoen.com • Tea by the pot. Afternoon set tea. A la carte menu. $$

77

Mark's at the Mark Hotel
25 E. 77th St. at Madison Ave.

Polished wood walls, gold-leaf edged moldings, Italian marble, tables set on two terraced levels with wrought-iron railings, and rich, muted tones of burgundy, rose and teal contribute to the Mark's elegant atmosphere. Tea Master Ringo Lo, formerly associated with the Peninsula Hotel in Hong Kong, and Le Crillon in Paris, was coaxed out of retirement to preside over the Mark's tea service.

Three different tea services are available: *The Mark's Tea* offers homemade raisin scones with buttery mascarpone cheese and fruit preserves, tea sandwiches filled with smoked salmon, Louisiana prawns with roasted-pepper relish, miniature tea pastries and a large selection of international teas. *The Strawberry Cream Tea* replaces pastries with fresh berries and crème Chantilly. *The Mandarin Tea* showcases fine, hand-picked and processed Chinese teas.

Master Lo is on hand for afternoon tea, and once a month, he teaches a two-hour class on *The Art of Chinese Tea*. The benefits and pleasures of drinking tea are discussed before attendees learn about six general categories – light green, dark green, yellow, black, white and aged tea as well as five types of flowering teas. Presiding over a polished tea trolley, Lo uses a tea spade to scoop the loose leaves and deposit them in the *chappei*, a small Yixing clay pot.

Each tea's ideal water temperature is described, and brewed in a glass pot; guests can observe the difference between "shrimp eye" and "fish eye" size bubbles. A variety of freshly made dim sum dumplings and Asian-inspired sweets are served with the teas sampled. Students are given a written handout to help remind them of Lo's tips, but his best advice is: "Every day drink, drink, taste, ask questions, and make a mess!"

• Daily 2:30-5:30pm • Subway: 6 train to 77th St. • Tel. 212-879-1864 • Major credit cards • www.mandarinoriental.com • Tea by the pot. Afternoon set tea. Cream tea. Tea-tasting class. $$

Lady M Cake Boutique
41 E. 78th St. btwn. Park and Madison Aves.

Originally a supplier for high-end restaurants and gourmet shops, the boutique went public with a twelve-seat café in December of 2004. The crisp white shop is as light and airy as the delectable desserts displayed on the 24-foot long, marble-topped pastry case. White chairs cluster around tiny tables set on curlicue bases. Loose tea, carefully brewed by your server with an eye on a timer, is served in sand-colored, hand-painted Limoges china pots. You may choose from *Creamy Morning*, a black tea with caramel notes, *Chai Berry, Green Splendor, Lady M Grey,* Assam, and an herbal blend.

The New York Times raved about Lady M's *Mille Crepes* cake – twenty layers of crepe separated by not-too-sweet whipped cream with a crème brulee-like caramelized top. There's a green-tea version, too. Tea lovers will also enjoy the green tea éclair and the Earl Grey mousse sponge cake among 29 other varieties. A selection of gourmet grilled panini sandwiches and gelati are available.

• Mon.-Sat. 9am-8pm, Sun. 10am-6pm • Subway: 6 train to 77th St. • Tel. 212-452-2222 • Reservations not accepted • Major credit cards • www.ladymconfections.com • Tea by the pot. Sandwiches. Snacks. Sweets. $

The Pembroke Room at the Lowell Hotel
28 E. 63rd St. btwn. Park & Madison Aves.

Secluded in a serene second-floor setting, the Pembroke Room is identified only by discreet letters etched on the mahogany door's frosted glass panel. Lavish swaths of polished chintz, gilt mirrors, a needlepoint carpet, and Chinese porcelains heighten the aristocratic atmosphere. Twenty varieties of loose tea are offered along with scones, Devonshire cream, seasonal berries, finger sandwiches, and pastries served on hand-painted Pickard china.

• Daily 3-6pm • Subway: F train to Lexington Ave. at 63rd St. • Tel. 212-838-1400 • www.lowellhotel.com • Reservations recommended • Afternoon set tea. A la carte menu. $$$

The Petrie Court Café at the Metropolitan Museum of Art
1000 Fifth Ave. at 82nd St.

The Metropolitan Museum of Art was founded in 1870 with funds from civic leaders and businessmen who believed that a museum would be a gift to the city as well as a boon for business. Today, over two million works of art make the museum New York's

The Metropolitan Museum of Art was founded in 1870 with funds from civic leaders and businessmen. Today, over two million works of art make the museum New York's number one tourist attraction.

number one tourist attraction. The gift shop sells several styles of ceramic teapots, cup and saucer sets, as well as tea books.

The European-style, table-service café is located on the first floor in the Petrie Sculpture Court. The floor-to-ceiling glass wall gives a stunning view of Central Park. The menu changes to reflect current exhibitions. During the House of Chanel fashion exhibit, a Continental-style afternoon tea was served on a tiered stand. Tiny finger sandwiches included smoked salmon, tarragon-shrimp salad, cucumber and watercress, and a curried mango-chicken salad. Miniature scones or toast triangles accompanied by Devonshire cream, lemon curd, fruit preserves, petits fours, and fruit tartlets completed the treats. The bagged tea selection includes six basic blacks and blends, two greens, and three herbal infusions. Tea is served in two-cup ceramic pots.

• Open only to museum visitors. Closed Mondays. Afternoon Tea served Sun., Tues., Thurs. 2:30-4:30pm, Fri.-Sat. 2:30-5pm • Subway: 4/5/6 trains to 86th St. • Tel. 212-570-3964 • Reservations required for parties of five or more • Major credit cards • www.metmuseum.org • Afternoon set tea. Tea by the pot. $

Sarabeth's Restaurant
1295 Madison Ave. btwn. 92nd & 93rd Sts.

Acclaimed pastry chef and award-winning jam maker Sarabeth Levine opened a tiny bakery-kitchen in 1981. The success of her family's 200-year-old marmalade recipe and home-style baked goods spawned four restaurants. Three locations serve a scrumptious afternoon tea. See flagship listing on page 89.

• Afternoon tea: Mon.-Fri. 3:30-5:30pm • Subway: 4/5/6 trains to 86th St. • Tel. 212-410-7335 • Reservations not accepted • Child friendly • Major credit cards

• www.sarabeth.com • Tea by the pot. Afternoon tea. A la carte menu. $

Urasenke Chanoyu Center
153 E. 69th St. btwn. Lexington &Third Aves.

The Urasenke Chanoyu Center, part of an international network devoted to teaching the art of tea, is hidden in a Victorian carriage house that was once the studio of painter Mark Rothko. Hisashi Yamada, a master of the Way of Tea Chanoyu, was born in Japan and came to New York in 1964 to lecture at the World's Fair. As center director, he teaches a ten-lesson course and hosts a monthly open house during which guests may experience a short tea ceremony.

Attendees remove their shoes at the door and wait quietly in the library until invited to walk through a tree-filled courtyard overlooking a Zen rock garden. Their destination is one of the tea rooms, built according to traditional guidelines by Japanese craftsmen with imported materials. Seated on tatami mats, guests listen to an overview of the 16th-century ritual and are coached in proper etiquette before being given a cup of matcha green tea and a seasonal sweet. The choreographed gestures contribute to the meditative experience encouraging participants to live in the moment. Many people report feeling a sense of communion and calm that sustains them when they return to the "world of delusion."

• Closed Sun.-Mon. Hours: Tues.-Wed. and Fri. 9am-5pm, Sat. 9am-noon • Subway: 6 train to 68th St. at Hunter College • Tel. 212-988-6161 • Reservations required. • Tea seminar $. Chanoyu lessons $$

Shopping Sites for Tea Lovers

Ages Past
450 E. 78th St. btwn. York and First Aves.

This charming barn-red clapboard building houses a small shop that stocks 19th-century English ceramics, including early Wedgwood, canary ware, luster ware, and transfer ware. Store specialty: china commemorating royal weddings and coronations.
• Mon.-Sat. 11am-5pm (call to confirm hours) • Subway: 6 train to 77th St. • Tel. 212-628-0725

Seated on tatami mats, guests at the Urasenke Chanoyu Center listen to an overview of the 16th-century tea ritual and are coached in proper etiquette before being given a cup of matcha green tea and a seasonal sweet.

Bardith, Ltd.
901 Madison Ave. at 72nd St. (Tel. 212-737-3775) and 31 E. 72nd St. bet. Madison and Park Aves. (Tel. 212-737-8660)

Both stores stock exquisite, museum-quality English, European, and Chinese ceramics – porcelain, Dutch delft and faience –

dating from the late 17th to 19th centuries. Dinnerware, partial and full tea sets, and orphaned cups and saucers are available.
• Mon.-Fri. 11am-5:30pm • Cash or check only

Barney's Chelsea Passage
660 Madison Ave. at 61st St.

Chelsea Passage is located on Barney's ninth floor and offers chic tableware, including boldly decorated Missoni porcelain tea pots, Alessi kettles designed by architect Michael Graves, and more traditional pieces from Bernardaud.
• Mon.-Fri. 10am-8pm, Sat. 10am-7pm. Sun. 11am-6pm • Subway: 4/5/6/N/R/W trains to 59th St. at Lexington Ave.; N/R trains to Fifth Ave. • Tel. 212-826-8900 • Major credit cards

Eli's Manhattan
1411 Third Ave. at 80th St.

Eli is the son of the original Mr. Zabar, and his passion for perfection is well known. With groceries in his genes, Eli operates an artisanal bread bakery, a catering business, gift shop, restaurant, wine boutique, and markets. At most locations, you may purchase a cup of bagged tea to sip with your freshly baked brownie, or a piece of shortbread made from his mother's recipe. Standard English and Irish teas, loose and bagged, and loose teas from Golden Moon and Heidard are stocked. Teatime gift baskets contain some of Eli's popular baked goods, jams and honey, and a selection of teas from Taylors of Harrogate and Bewley's.
• Daily 7am-9pm • Subway: 4/5/6 trains to 86th St. • Tel. 212-717-8100 • Major credit cards • www.elizabar.com

Eli's Vinegar Factory
431 E. 91st. St. btwn. 1st and York Ave.

There's a small housewares department here with tea making supplies, but the focus is on gourmet food. Bagged and boxed teas are available plus loose leaves from Twinings, Harney and Sons, Heidard, The Highland Tea Company, Golden Moon, and a dozen of Eli's own blends.
• Daily 7am-9pm; upstairs dining area open weekends 8am-4pm • Subway: 4/5/6 trains to 86th St. • Tel. 212-987-0885

Gourmet Garage
301 E. 64th St. btwn. 1st and 2nd Aves.

This warehouse-style grocery chain carries a good selection of honey, jams, packaged cookies, and standard bagged and loose teas: Taylors of Harrogate, Twinings, and Tazo as well as healthful Traditional Medicinals. Multiple locations.
• Daily 7am-10pm • Subway: 4/5/6/F/N/

(continued on page 84)

With groceries in his genes, Eli Zabar operates an artisanal bread bakery, a catering business, gift shop, restaurant, wine boutique, and markets. His passion for perfection is well known.

Payard Patisserie and Bistro

1032 Lexington Ave. btwn. 73rd and 74th Sts.

Francois Payard is a third-generation, French-born pasty chef. After honing his skills in his grandfather's acclaimed Riviera shop, Payard starred in three and four-star restaurants in Paris and New York. The James Beard Association named him Pastry Chef of the Year, as did the *Bon Appetit* Food and Entertainment Awards. Payard Patisserie and Bistro was established in 1997 to share his passion for pastry and hand-sculpted chocolates.

Pause to admire the artfully crafted pastries, savories, and decadent desserts in the glass cases before proceeding to the dining room. The bistro's warm colors, mahogany woodwork, colorfully striped banquettes, glittering mirrors, and amber glass lighting evoke a feeling of a shop on Paris' Left Bank.

Payard serves and sells its signature tea. Loose tea is brewed by the pot; the house blend is a black tea with citrus accents. *Le Thè* is presented on a three-tiered server. Scones and melt-in-your-mouth madeleines are served with *crème Chantilly* and homemade confiture. Sophisticated and scrumptious sandwiches include a pretzel with salmon *rillette* and chive-cream cheese, *vitello tonnato* (veal and pureed tuna) on *Ciabatta* bread, and a miniature Mediterranean *pan bagnat*. A tasting of tiny pastries include a *sacher* (dark chocolate ganache with raspberry filling), pistachio, raspberry, and hibiscus-infused mousse tarts, coffee and chocolate éclairs, and an assortment of *macarons* and chocolate truffles. *Le Thè Royal* adds a flute of Paul Goerg champagne with a splash of kir. Caviar and blinis enrich the savories. Payard also caters off-site tea parties for up to three hundred people.

• Tea time Mon.-Sat. 3:30-5pm • Subway: 6 train to 77th St. • Tel. 212-717-5252 • Reservations required • Major credit cards • www.payard.com • Tea by the pot. Afternoon set tea. A la carte menu. $ $

83

R/W trains to 59th St. Lexington Ave. • Tel. 212-535-6271 • Major credit cards • www.gourmetgarage.com

Grace's Marketplace
1237 3rd Ave. btwn. 71st and 72nd Sts.

Grace Balducci Doria began her food career at age ten working in her parents' Greenwich Village store. Grace's own store is known for outstanding service and an extraordinary selection of fine foods, including picture-perfect pastries. The Grace Tea company, no relation, supplies 12 classic loose tea selections; there are bagged teas from Bigelow, Kusmi, Pompadour, Salada, Stash and Typhoo.
• Mon.-Sat. 7am-8:30pm, Sun 8am-7pm • Subway: 6 train to 68th St. • www.gracesmarketplace.com • Tel. 212-737-0600 • Major credit cards

Gracious Home
1220 Third Ave at 70th St.

This family-owned store stocks twenty different styles of tea kettles, including a solid-copper whistling English Simplex as well as several electric versions. Cast iron teapots and ceramic styles with matching mugs, cups, and saucers are available. Additional location Upper West Side.
• Mon.-Fri. 8am-7pm, Sat. 9am-7pm, Sun. 10am-6pm • Subway: 6 train to 68th St. Hunter College • Tel. 212-517-6300 • www.gracioushome.com • Major credit cards

Hadley Antiques, Ltd.
1026 Lexington Ave. btwn. 73rd & 74th Sts.

Just a few doors from Payard Patisserie and La Terrine, Hadley's stocks a lovely assortment of antique cut-glass and silver English biscuit barrels, sterling curate stands, candlesticks, trays, and other tea table niceties.
• Closed summer Saturdays. Open Mon.-Sat. 11am-5pm • Subway: 6 train to 77th St. • Tel. 212-535-7002 • Major credit cards

La Terrine
1024 Lexington Ave. at 73rd St.

La Terrine stocks colorful hand-painted French, Italian, and Portuguese pottery including a variety of teapots and mugs. There's *Quimper* and *Rafaelesco* plus patterns from lesser known factories and pretty Provencal linens.
• Mon.-Tue. and Thur., 10:30am-5pm; Wed., Fri.-Sun. 10:30am-6pm • Subway: 6 train to 77th St. • Tel. 212-988-3366 • Major credit cards

Grace Balducci Doria (Grace's Marketplace) began her food career at age ten working in her parents' Greenwich Village store. Grace's own store is known for outstanding service and an extraordinary selection of fine foods, including picture-perfect pastries.

M. Rohrs' House of Fine Teas and Coffees
303 E. 85th St. btwn. 1st and 2nd Aves.

Mary Rohrs opened a shop selling fine tea and coffee in 1896. It's still there. Over 90 teas are stocked, some in the original red tins, others in glass jars. Thirty loose teas include Assam, Rohrs' Summer Brew, Russian Georgian, and a Japanese pan-fired green. There are packaged teas from Benchley, The Boston Company, Foojoy, Fortnum & Mason, and many others. The store carries ceramic pots, a wide array of tea infusers and tea balls, and tea-themed gift baskets. Four flavors of mouthwatering rugelach made especially for Rohrs', scones, and other snacks may be enjoyed with a cup of tea while seated at the counter or in one of the cast-off chairs plunked next to the fish tank.

• Daily 6am-10pm • Subway: 4/5/6 trains to 86 St. • Tel. 212-396-4456 • Major credit cards • www.rohrs.com

Sara
952 Lexington Ave. btwn. 69th & 70th Sts.

Sara is Japanese for ceramic, and this store imports teapots, cups, serving dishes, and decorative accessories directly from Japan. They also carry the work of contemporary American potters.

• Mon.-Fri. 11am-7pm, Sat. noon-6pm • Subway: 6 train to 68th St., Hunter College • Tel. 212-772-3243 • Major credit cards • www.saranyc.com

William-Wayne and Company
850 Lexington Ave. btwn. 64th & 65th Sts.

Shop here for an eclectic mix of vintage and contemporary tableware, linens and decorative accessories including a good selection of handsome trays, tea tables, tin ware and lovely paper napkins for picnics. Second location in Greenwich Village; see listing on page 34.

• Closed Sundays. Hours: Mon.-Sat. 10:30am-6:30pm • Subway: F train to Lexington Ave. • Tel. 212-288-9243

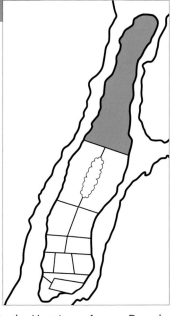

Harlem
and Upper
Manhattan

Native Americans lived on the land ten miles north of Manhattan's tip when the Dutch arrived and named it *Nieuw Haarlem*. Country estates gave way to gracious brownstones, then high-rise apartments, home to European immigrants, African-Americans, and West Indians. Artists, writers, and intellectuals – Zora Neale Hurston, Aaron Douglas, and Marcus Garvey – contributed to the Harlem Renaissance. Duke Ellington, Dizzy Gillespie, Lena Horne, and Charlie Parker made the joint jump. After years of decline, Harlem is flourishing again.

The Harlem Tea Room
1793-A Madison Ave., NE corner 118th St.

Harlem native Patrice Clayton, a lifelong tea-lover, opened the Harlem Tea Room in 2004. Designed to promote interaction between community residents and visitors from the tri-state area, the space hosts poetry readings and book signings, musical events, art shows, and seminars. The contemporary décor is warmed by floor-length burgundy curtains, a copper tea bar, and paisley-patterned upholstery. "It's a place where people can relax and feel comfortable outside their home," Patrice says.

Twenty-one types of teas, including chai, organics, herbals, and three exotic blends, are on the menu. A three-course afternoon tea is offered every Saturday (1-4pm) by reservation only. Guests are served scones, standard tea sandwiches, and assorted desserts. A pot of tea and a slice of bourbon pecan pie or a grilled "Uptown-Melt" sandwich are always on offer. Children's tea parties and catered "tea parties-to-go" are available.

• Closed Mon. Hours: Tues.-Thur. 10am-9pm, Fri. 10am-10pm, Sat. 9am-10pm, Sun. 9am-7:30pm. • Subway: 2/3/6 trains to 116th St. • www.harlemtearoom.com •Tel. 212-348-3471 • Reservations required. • Major credit cards • Tea by the pot. Afternoon set tea. Cream tea. A la carte menu. $

Getting to Know Harlem: Things to Do, Places to Go

The Morris-Jumel Mansion
W. 161st St. and Jumel Terrace

George Washington slept and sipped tea here in 1776.
• Wed.-Sun. 10am-4pm • Subway: C train to 163rd St. at Amsterdam Ave. • Tel. 212-923-8008 • www.morrisjumel.org

The Studio Museum of Harlem
144 W. 125th St. btwn. Lenox Ave. and Adam Clayton Powell Blvd. (7th Ave.)

African, African-American and Caribbean art and artifacts.
• Closed Mon.-Tues. and major holidays. Hours: Wed.-Fri. and Sun. noon-6pm, Sat. 10am-6pm • Subway: A/B/C/D/2/3 trains to 125th St. • www.studiomuseum.org • Tel. 212-864-4500

The Harlem Week/ Harlem Jazz and Music Festival is an annual summer event featuring food tastings, live music, art exhibits, street fairs, and sporting events.

Upper West Side

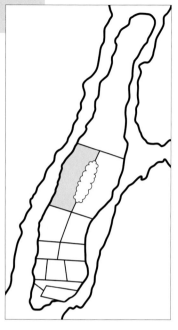

The Upper West Side runs north of Columbus Circle, claiming everything west of Central Park and up to Harlem. Less rarefied than the East Side, actors, writers, musicians, media moguls, celebrities, and families mingle comfortably and enjoy performances at Lincoln Center or visits to the Cathedral of St. John the Divine.

Leaf Storm Tea

176 W. 94th St., corner 94th St. and Amsterdam Ave.

Leaf Storm is the romantic name of New York's tiniest tea room, a walk-up counter in a walk-around town. Amy Chen grew up in a tea-drinking family, but the children's clothing designer got an MBA before changing careers. Amy decided to open a tea room with the ambience of a 1920's Shanghai jazz club, and she spent five years visiting Chinese tea plantations to educate herself. "The scent of oolong tea leaves drying in the air is what heaven must smell like," says Chen.

Three years of searching for an affordable space left her empty-handed. But one day, right in her own neighborhood, Amy spotted a "bump-out" attached to the side of another building. Creative renovation turned the 80-square feet into a Manhattan drive-thru for tea. The diminutive shop stocks 35 types of liquid treasure: white tea, black, flavored black, oolong, green, flavored green, herbals, and fruit, stored in shiny tins similar to those found in Chinese herbal medicine shops.

Located across the street from a school, Leaf Storm caters to moms and their youngsters, dog-walkers, bikers, and folks heading off to work. Ms. Chen brews loose leaves by the cup, using a disposable pouch, so busy people can take their tea to-go. In warm weather, little tables are set out for sidewalk sippers. In winter, loyal patrons cheerfully line up to place orders at the sliding glass window, where tea and treats are served with a smile. Amy's delectable hot chocolate made with peppermint tea is a best seller. Packaged tea and attractive sampler kits, with ten different teas in two sizes, are sold for home brewing.

- Mon.-Fri. 7:30am-5pm, Sat. 8:30am-5pm
- Subway: B/C trains to 96th St. • Tel. 212-222-3300 • Cash only • Tea by the cup. Snacks. $

Sarabeth's Restaurant

423 Amsterdam Ave. btwn. 80th & 81st Sts. and 40 Central Park S. btwn. 5th & 6th Aves

Sarabeth Levine, a James Beard-acclaimed pastry chef and award-winning jam maker, opened a tiny bakery-kitchen in 1981.The success of her family's 200-year-old marmalade recipe and home-style baked goods spawned four restaurants that serve breakfast, lunch, and brunch. Three locations serve a scrumptious afternoon tea. You may choose an assortment of finger sandwiches – smoked salmon with cucumber-cream

(continued on page 91)

"Alice fell down the rabbit hole, but you'll only have to duck down a short flight of stairs to reach this cheerful tea room."

Alice's Tea Cup
102 W. 73rd St. off Columbus Ave.

Alice fell down the rabbit hole, but you'll only have to duck down a short flight of stairs to reach this cheerful tea room. Cream-colored walls are decorated with whimsical quotes including "Teatime is quiet time. Off with your cell phone or off with your head!" Guests may choose from 120 types of loose tea served in china pots.

Four scrumptious set teas are offered, all with generous portions: The Nibble: Pot of tea, choice of scone with preserves and cream, choice of sandwich, dessert sampling. The Mad Hatter: Pot of tea, choice of scone, preserves and cream, unlimited sandwiches, Jean's "not-yet-but soon-to-be-famous" mocha-chocolate-chip cake or a tea-infused fruit tart or chai crème brulee with a selection of cookies. The Jabberwocky: All of the above with the cake, crème brulee or tart, and cookies. The Wee Tea (ideal for children under ten): Choice of herbal or fruit tisane, half a scone with preserves, cream, choice of sandwich, and white rabbit dark-chocolate mousse with milk chocolate shavings. There's also a pureed baby food entrée of the day.

Sandwiches are tasty and more imaginative than the standard fare – an olive tapenade with goat cheese and roasted cumin-carrots on semolina bread, or a lapsang souchong smoked-chicken breast with Granny Smith apple and herbed-goat cheese on seven–grain bread. Grilled sandwiches, soups, and salads are also available.

Sweets and treats include chai crème brulee, mocha-chocolate-chip cake, Vervaine tea-infused lemon tart, assorted cookies with or without raspberry-mint tea sorbet or Tahitian vanilla gelato, warm chocolate cake, chocolate mousse, s'mores, mixed berries with homemade Chantilly crème and lavender honey, or a vanilla ice cream sandwich served on a freshly-baked cookie (peanut-butter-chocolate chip or oatmeal-raisin). The retail area has a large assortment of loose teas and herbal tisanes, teapots, cosies, strainers, brewing accessories, books about tea, fairies, and fun.

• Mon.-Thurs. 8am-8pm, Fri. 8am-10pm, Sat. 10am-10pm, Sun. 10am-8pm • Subway: 1 train to 72nd St. Amsterdam Ave.; B/C trains to Central Park West (Second location on Upper East Side) • Tel. 212-799-3006 • Reservations required for parties of six or more • Child friendly • Major credit cards • www.alicesteacup.com • Tea by the pot. Afternoon set tea. A la carte menu. $$

cheese and fresh mint, chicken salad on raisin-walnut bread, radish-cucumber with cream cheese, and a Black Forest ham and brie – with a pot of freshly brewed tea. Those with a sweet tooth add cookies and currant scones served with fruit preserves and "clabber" cream. You may drop in anytime for a slice of Budapest cake, lemon pound cake, chocolate souffle, warm berry-bread pudding, or a crème brulee ginger-pecan tart with a choice of ten types of tea. Additional Upper East Side location.

• Afternoon tea: Mon.-Fri. 3:30pm-5:30pm • Subway to Amsterdam Ave.: 1 train to 79th St., Broadway (Tel. 212-496-6280) • Subway to Central Park location: A/B/C/D/1 trains to 59th St. Columbus Cir., N/R/W trains to 5th Ave. 59th St. (Tel: 212-826-5959) • Reservations not accepted • Child friendly • Major credit cards • www.sarabeth.com • Tea by the pot. Afternoon set tea. A la carte menu. $

The Sky Lobby Lounge at the Mandarin Oriental Hotel
80 Columbus Circle at 60th St.

Located on the 35th floor, the Sky Lobby Lounge's wall of windows affords a breathtaking view of Central Park and the city skyline. The room is furnished in a muted pale gold and brown palette, blending modern design and oriental flair. The afternoon tea service presents a selection of traditional and Asian-inspired treats, sweets, and the Mandarin Oriental's signature ginger scones served with Devon cream and homemade marmalade. Choose from a selection of Tealeaves tea brewed by the pot. There are four herbal infusions, three greens, an oolong, and four black blends. Mandarin Blossom, a Chinese green tea perfumed with the essence of fresh mandarin oranges, and Mandarin Oolong, scented with mandarin orange and a hint of vanilla bean, are the hotel's signature blends.

SUBMITTED PHOTO

Three delectable hot chocolates – Mandarin Oriental Hot White Chocolate by Jacques Torres, a chili-spiced concoction, and a traditional brew – are available. Exotic desserts include cheesecake with a raspberry-*yuzu* (Japanese citrus) compote, a mango rice pudding tart, and a coconut-lime rice pudding.

• Daily 2:30-4:30pm • Subway: A/B/C/D/1 trains to Columbus Cir. • Tel. 212-805-8800 • Reservations accepted only for hotel guests • Major credit cards • www.mandarinoriental.com/newyork • Tea by the pot. Afternoon set tea. A la carte menu. $$$

Shopping Sites for Tea Lovers

Empire Coffee & Tea Company
568 Ninth Ave. btwn. 41st and 42nd Sts.

Located half a block from the Port Authority bus terminal, this historic (1908) shop stocks coffee and more than 60 loose-leaf teas. Among them: Chunmee green, Java Superior, Rose Black, Russian Wine, and Yunnan Black Mainland. Herbal infusions and boxed teabags are available, along with kettles, teapots, mugs, and infusers.
• Mon.-Fri. 8am-7pm, Sat. 9am-6:30pm, Sun. 1am-5pm • Tel. 212- 268-1220 • www.empirecoffeetea.com • Major credit cards

Gourmet Garage
2567 Broadway at 96th St.

This warehouse-style grocery chain stocks bagged and loose tea as well as honey, jam, and tea time treats. Multiple locations. See flagship listing on page 82.
• Daily 7am-10pm • Subway: 1/2/3 trains to 96th St. • Tel. 212-663-0656 • Major credit cards • www.gourmetgarage.com

Gracious Home
1992 Broadway at 67th St.

Gracious Home is a family-owned store with an impressive assortment of tea kettles, teapots, cups and mugs. See flagship listing on page 84.
• Mon.-Sat. 9am- 9pm, Sun. 10am-7pm
• Subway: 1 train to 66th St. Lincoln Center • Tel. 212-231-7800

Maya Schaper Cheese and Antiques
106 W. 69th St. btwn. Columbus Ave. and Broadway

Cheese and antiques seem an odd combination, but Maya Schaper dearly loves both. On one side of her shop, gourmet cheese is stored in refrigerated cases and the wooden counter brims with baskets of baked goods such as brownies and buttery apricot bars. Just opposite, floor-to-ceiling shelves are crammed with antique and vintage teapots, cups, dessert plates, wooden-handled bread knives, silver sugar tongs, brass toasting forks, tea napkins, towels, and the occasional cosy. Taylors of Harrogate loose tea and Stash bagged tea are sold here.
• Daily 10am-8pm • Subway: B/C trains to 72nd St. • Tel. 212-873-2100 • Major credit cards

Oren's Daily Roast
2882 Broadway btwn. 112th and 113th Sts.

This chain is dedicated to delivering roasted coffee but also stocks up to 25 loose teas

and sells boxed bagged tea, cast-iron, glass and ceramic teapots, colorful mugs, and brewing accessories.
• Mon.-Fri. 8am-9pm, Sat.-Sun. 9am-8pm
• Subway: 1 train to 110th St. • Tel. 212-749-8779 • Major credit cards •
www.orensdailyroast.com

Sensuous Bean
66 W. 70th St. btwn. Columbus Ave. and Central Park West

This small shop is known for its coffee but also stocks a large variety of loose teas in glass jars. The 19 blacks include Choice Darjeeling Long TGFOP Makaibari Estate, Nilgiri certified 100% organic tea from the Korakundah Estate, Kenya Michimukuru, and the provocative Sensuous Breakfast. There are 19 flavored blacks, fifteen greens including a pan-fired Imperial Green, and many herbal tisanes and boxed bagged teas.
• Mon. 8:30am-7pm, Tues.-Wed. 8:30am-6pm, Thurs.-Fri. 8:30am-6:45pm, Sat. 8:30am-6pm, Sun. 9:30am-6pm • Subway: B/C trains to 72nd St. • Tel. 212-724-7725 • www.sensuousbean.com • Major credit cards

Whole Foods Market
Shops at Columbus Circle, 10 Columbus Cir. btwn. 58th and 60th Sts.

Specialty loose tea supplied by Rishi and In Pursuit of Tea, properly packaged in light and air-tight containers. Boxed and bagged standards as well as honey, jam, pastries, and other treats. Multiple locations.
• Daily 8am-10pm • Subway: A/B/C/D/1 train to 59th St. Columbus Circle • Tel. 212-823-9600 • Major credit cards •
www.wholefoodsmarket.com

Zabar's
2245 Broadway btwn. 80th and 81st Sts.

Estabished in 1934 to sell smoked fish, Zabar's now is known for the fabulous cheese counter, deli, baked goods, chocolates, candies, condiments, and prepared foods. Loose tea from Grace Tea, Serendipitea, Kusmi, Twinings, Two Leaves and a Bud, and other brands are displayed next to a huge selection of honey and jams – 27 types from Tiptree alone. There's the usual assortment of boxed bagged teas, plus selections from the Dublin Tea company and chai latte mixes. Upstairs, the housewares department carries electric and stove-top tea kettles in a dozen colors, plus cast iron, ceramic, and glass teapots. To aid brewing, the store stocks water filters, tea scoops, infusers, and several thermos styles.
• Subway: 1 train to 79th St. • Tel. 212-787-2000 • www.zabars.com • Major credit cards

Brooklyn

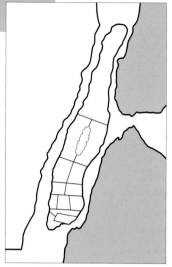

The Canarsee Indians lived on the land Dutch settlers named *Breuckelen* ("broken land"). Located on the southwestern tip of Long Island, Brooklyn would be the fourth-largest city in the country if it were not part of New York City. You can get there by subway or walk across the historic Brooklyn Bridge for a spectacular skyline view of Manhattan.

Brighton Beach, located on Brooklyn's Coney Island peninsula, is home to the largest Russian enclave in the United States. A subway can whisk you from Manhattan, in under an hour, to Brighton Beach Avenue where homesick émigrés and serious foodies shop for tea, samovars, and other Russian specialties. Little English is spoken here. Shop clerks are often glum and sometimes rude, but that's part of the experience, if not the charm.

Gina's Café

409 Brighton Beach Ave. btwn. Fourth and Fifth Sts. (Brighton Beach)

Gina's Café is a cheerful spot to sit and sip Russian-style tea (Wissotzky teabags) with lemon and jam. Cafe owner Gina Sharon, who hales from Ukraine, prides herself on the smoked salmon and red caviar salad, but there is a good variety of *knishes, pelmeni,* and *vareneki* as well as blintzes, crepes, and pastries to savor with Russian ice cream.

• Daily 11am-11pm • Subway: B/Q trains to Brighton Beach • Tel. 718-646-6297 • Credit card minimum order $10 • Tea by the pot. Full menu and a la carte dishes. $

In Pursuit of Tea, the company founded by Sebastian Beckwith and Alexander Scott, is Brooklyn-based, and that bodes well for tea fans.

Sweet Melissa Patisserie

276 Court St. btwn. Butler and Douglass Sts. (Cobble Hill)

French Culinary Institute graduate Melissa Murphy Hagenbart knows how to bake a fancy French tart but is just as happy making classic American desserts and gourmet granola. She made a name for herself baking for upscale Manhattan restaurants but decided to open a patisserie in an affordable neighborhood.

The Cobble Hill storefront is dominated by a glass pastry case where colorful petits fours gleam like jewels. Locals line up to snap up the sticky buns, biscotti, twice-baked brioche, and sweet or savory muffins and croissants. The little tea room is cheerfully decorated with French country flair: upholstered banquettes lined with teacup print fabric and pumpkin-colored walls hung with vintage posters advertising French chocolate. A shaded garden offers additional seating in good weather.

Loose tea (seven standards, a decaf, and three herbals) is available brewed by the pot and served with a metal strainer. Tea-time treats include fabulous sour-cherry scones served with raspberry-currant jam, a salmon, dill-crème cheese roll, puff pastry filled with curried chicken, and quiche. Hazelnut petits fours with apricot filling, passion fruit tartlets, chestnut-honey madeleines, and jam-filled roasted pistachio thumbprint cookies are some of the sweets offered. If you can't wait for afternoon tea, stop in for a bowl of granola made with oats, almonds, whole-grain flakes, sunflower and pumpkin seeds baked with honey and spices, and a pot of breakfast tea. Second location in SoHo. See listing page 27.

Cobble Hill, a residential neighborhood south of Brooklyn Heights, is a New York City historic district dotted with restored townhouses and small, one-of-a-kind shops.

95

• Afternoon tea served daily 11am-5pm •
Subway: F/G trains to Bergen St. • Tel. 718-
855-3410 • Child friendly • Major credit
cards • www.sweetmelissapatisserie.com
• Tea by the pot. Full afternoon tea. Snacks.
Sweets. $

The Tea Lounge
*837 Union St. btwn. 6th and 7th Seventh
Aves. and 350 7th Ave. (Park Slope)*

Neither of these Park Slope locations is your
granny's tea room. An art gallery, free wireless internet access, weekly story hours,
sing-alongs, live music and other special
events make the main location a community center. Open the door to the former
warehouse, and you'll spy dozens of people
sprawled on the collection of castoff
couches and chairs. Some are sleeping,
others hunch over laptops, books, or a chess
board. Three women discuss a script. A
photographer flips through a model's port-
folio. Young mothers, babes-in-arms, meet
weekly to trade teething tips over cups of
tea.

Nearly 80 loose leaf teas are offered –
blacks, greens, whites, blends such as Persian Peach, Rosey Earl, green tea, blood-
orange and pear, four types of chai, fruit and
herbal mixes, as well as Rooibos,
honeybush, and yerba mate. The T.L. Kids'
blend is a fruit mélange especially formu-
lated without flavored oils. Most teas are
organic and available in bulk, or by the pot.

You place your order at the bakery counter
stacked with snacks. A salesperson uses a
long tailed spoon to scoop loose tea leaves,
from a divided drawer, for you to see and

*The Park Slope
neighborhood
stretches from the
Gowanus Canal to
Prospect Park. Once
populated with Irish
and Italian laborers,
Park Slope's
renovated row
houses and beautiful
brownstones are
now home to urbane
professionals,
writers, and
families.*

Russian Tea Traditions

Russia's love for tea began in the 17th century when a Chinese envoy gifted the Czar with a tea chest. Camel caravans soon trekked the Silk Road carrying costly Chinese silks and tea to trade for furs. Eventually, the price of tea fell and all levels of Russian society adopted the beverage.

After supper, in country and city, families gather around a table set with a shiny samovar, a metal, urn-shaped vessel, modeled on the traditional Tibetan hot pot. A small teapot filled with a tea concentrate is placed on top to stay warm. The concentrate is poured into teacups or glasses and diluted to taste with hot water from the samovar's spigot. Up to 40 cups may be prepared this way.

Long ago, coal or wood heated the urn, but today electric versions brew Russia's most popular non-alcoholic beverage. Tea is typically drunk after, but not during, meals. A mid-afternoon tea break might include *blinis* (buckwheat pancakes) slathered with jam, cottage cheese pudding, and other sweets.

The full-bodied black tea favored by Russians is traditionally served with lemon and sweetened with honey, sugar, or fruit jam. It is the custom to tuck a sugar cube in the cheek or clamp it between teeth while sipping tea. Morning tea may be spiced with cloves, ginger root, or cinnamon and taken with hot milk. On festive occasions, vodka or brandy are added to make tea grog.

smell. Your choice will be served in a pot on a footed wood block with a wooden cup. Frothy tea lattes and tea-based cocktails, served at the full bar, offer tea with a twist.

• Mon.-Thur. 7am-1am, Fri. 7am-2am, Sat. 8am-2am, Sun. 8am-10am • Subway to Union St. location: Q train to 7th Ave; 2/3 trains to Grand Army Plaza; M/R trains to Union St. (Tel. 718-789-2762) • Subway to 7th Ave. location: F train to 7th Ave. at 10th St. (Tel. 718-768-4966) • www.tealoungeny.com • Major credit cards • Tea by the pot. Snacks. Sweets. $

Shopping Sites for Tea Lovers

Kalinka Gifts
402 Brighton Beach Ave. btwn 4th & 5th Sts. (Brighton Beach)

Shop here for ceramic or metal samovars, cobalt net pattern porcelain teapots, and a wide range of tableware and decorative accessories.
• Mon.-Sat. 10am-7:30pm, Sun. 11am-7pm • Subway: B/Q trains to Brighton Beach • Tel. 718-743-4546 • Major credit cards

The Sunset Park neighborhood is named for the park that offers sunset harbor views; this neighborhood is located in south Brooklyn, south of Park Slope. Although the area is largely Hispanic, it is also New York's fastest growing Chinatown.

Leaf and Bean
83 Seventh Ave. btwn. Berkeley Pl. and Union St. (Park Slope)

Long a favorite, Leaf and Bean carries nearly 50 loose leaf teas from around the world. All the classics are here as well as several white teas, flavored and decaffeinated blends, herbal tisanes and boxed bagged teas from the industry's best-known suppliers. There's a wonderful assortment of quirky, colorful tewares including *Bopla!* sophisticated Swiss china.
• Mon.-Fri. 9:30am-7:30pm, Sat. 9am-7pm, Sun. 11am-7pm • Subway: B/Q trains to 7th Ave. • Tel. 718-638-5791 • Major credit cards • www.leafnbean.com

M&I International Foods
249 Brighton Beach Ave. btwn. 1st and 2nd Sts. (Brighton Beach)

This two-story emporium, nearly as big as Mother Russia, was founded 26 years ago. Shop the first floor for rye bread, big and black as a bowling ball, along with salmon and caviar to make delicious tea sandwiches. Pick up *pirozhki*, baked or fried pies, filled with meat, vegetables, or fruit for a hearty high tea. Upstairs, the great-wall-of-tea displays loose leaves from 15 vendors including Ahmad, Kusmi, Pompadour, Twinings, and Wissotzky as well as 35 types of bagged teas. There's a good selection of herbal tisanes including linden, lime, rosehip, hibiscus, and black current. Dozens of exotic honeys and jars of jam, compotes, and preserves – all the standards as well as Romanian rose petal, Morello cherry, boysenberry, and chestnut – are offered. Overwhelmed? Head to the cafe, located on the same floor, to snack on *vareneki*, meat and cheese-filled dumplings.
• Daily 8am-10pm • Subway: B/Q trains to Brighton Beach • Tel. 718-615-1011 • Major credit cards

Ten Ren
5817 8th Ave. btwn. 58th and 59th Sts. (Sunset Park)

Multiple locations. See description page 16.
• Daily 10am-8pm • Subway: D/M/N/R trains to 59th St. • Tel.718-853-0660 • Major credit cards • Bubble tea. Tea by the cup • www.tenrenusa.com

Two for the Pot
200 Clinton St. btwn. Atlantic Ave. and State St. (Brooklyn Heights)

John McGill is the charming owner of Two For The Pot,

which stocks over 40 types of loose tea in glass jars, boxed bagged tea and herbal tisanes. In addition to Assam, Ceylon, and Darjeeling, there are teas from China, Japan, Kenya, and a tea from Wales. Several custom blends are on offer including two types of Earl Grey, Himalyan – a blend of Assam and Darjeeling – and a spice mélange. The shop also sells spices, sundries, British biscuits, and herbs along with a selection of pots and brewing accessories.
• Closed Mondays. Hours: Tues-Fri. Noon-7pm, Sat. 10 am-6pm, Sun. (Oct.-May) 1-5pm • Subway: 2/3/4/5/M/N/R/W trains to Borough Hall/Court St. • Tel. 718-855-8173 • Major credit cards

Vintage Food Corporation
287 Brighton Beach Ave. btwn. 2nd and 3rd Sts. (Brighton Beach)

Located just up the street from M&I, Vintage Food has an even bigger tea assortment – 60 types, including 15 loose leaf varieties from Ceylon, India, and China – Assam Golden Tippy Long Leaf, Earl and Lady Gray, Imperial Rose, to name but a few. A large selection of herbal tisanes – sage, linden, apple, peppermint, mixed fruit, and many types of dieter's teas are also available. It's hard to resist the Tweety tea package decorated with the cheeky cartoon character brandishing a cup of tenvitamin tea. Bakers and snackers will be tempted by the enormous assortment of raw, roasted, smoked and salty nuts, and seeds. There are also dried fruits - seven types of raisins, as well as dates, crabapples, cranberries, cherries (sweet and sour), strawberries, blueberries, pineapple, and papaya.
• Daily 8am-9pm • Subway: B/Q trains to Brighton Beach • Tel. 718-769-6674 • Major credit cards

General George Washington's Brooklyn Heights headquarters provided a spectacular view of lower Manhattan. New York's first suburb and first historic district has many 19th century townhouses, quaint and quirky shops and lovely tree-lined streets.

Brooklyn: Things to Do and Places to Go

Brooklyn Academy of Music
30 Lafayette Ave. off Flatbush Ave.
• Subway: 2/3/4/5/M/N/Q/R/W to Pacific St./Atlantic Ave. • Tel.718-636-4100 • www.bam.org

Brooklyn Botanic Garden
1000 Washington Ave. at Eastern Parkway
• Subway; Q to Prospect Park; 2/3 trains to Eastern Pkwy. Brooklyn Museum • Tel. 718-623-7200 • www.bbg.org

Brooklyn Museum of Art
200 Eastern Parkway
• Subway: 2/3 train to Eastern Parkway/Brooklyn Museum • Tel.718-638-5000 • Free fiirst Sat. of each month • www.brooklynmuseum.org

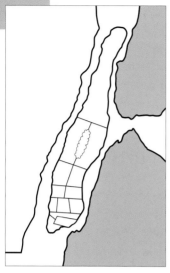

The Bronx

There's a lot to cheer in the Bronx: Yankee Stadium, a wonderful zoo, and botanical gardens, all accessible by subway or the Metro-North train from Grand Central Station. Come here, too, for a true Celtic tea and have your leaves read. Nearly one out of six Americans claim Celtic ancestors and in the 19th century, many Irish immigrants settled in New York. Katonah Avenue offers Irish eateries, bakeries, grocery stores, and news-agents that carry 80 different periodicals from the Emerald Isle. Hibernians like tea "strong enough to trot a mouse on," and typically take it with milk and sugar. If you'd like an authentic walnut-treacle scone or buttermilk-soda bread with your cuppa, just hop the subway to Woodlawn, in the Bronx.

The Irish Bakery Shop and Cafe
4268 Katonah Ave. corner of 235th St.

At this simple bakery-restaurant, you can order a hearty Irish breakfast – sausage, bacon, black and white pudding, broiled tomato, eggs any style, home fries, and home-made potato-bread toast – all day long for $8.95. Smaller appetites may be satisfied with freshly-baked soda bread, batch bread, pan loaf, or a couple of scones (raisin-walnut, mixed-fruit and coconut, plain brown or white – served toasted or not) with butter and jam,

accompanied by a mug of bagged Irish tea.
• Daily 8am-9pm • Tel. 718-994-0846
• Tea by the cup. A la carte and full menu. $

Rambling House
4292 Katonah Avenue at 236th St.

At Rambling House, there's a real Irish colleen, Roisin (pronounced Row-sheen), who'll read your tea leaves with a cup of Barry's Gold. An aunt, "who also had the gift," discovered Roisin's abilities when she was only five years old. While you're waiting your turn, order The Rambling House's high tea fare: shepherd's pie or fish and chips. Consider ordering the Katonah Avenue Favorite: bangers (Irish-style sausages), mashed potatoes, and baked beans washed down with a strong cup of tea. Reservations are required for a tea leaf reading by Roisin, who appears every other Wednesday evening 6-10pm. Cost is $30. Tel. 718-798-4510.

The Rambling House hosts tea leaf readings once each week by a gifted colleen.

• Daily 11:30am-2am; Sun. 11am-3pm • Subway: 4 train to Woodlawn station, then bus BX34 or Metro-North commuter rail to Woodlawn • Tel. 718-798-4510 • Major credit cards • www.ramblinghouse.com • Tea by the cup. Full menu. $

The Bronx: Things to Do and Places to Go

The **Bronx Zoo** is located at Fordham Road and the Bronx River Parkway, close to several subway stops; an express bus from Manhattan also stops at the zoo entrance. Visit www.bronxzoo.com for directions or call 718-367-1010.

SUBMITTED PHOTOS

The **New York Botanical Garden** is located at the Bronx River Parkway and Fordham Road. Take the Metro-North railroad's Harlem Local Line from Grand Central Terminal to the Botanical Garden Station - 22 minutes direct to the Garden gate. For information on Metro-North's discounted One-Day-Getaway to the Garden or for a train schedule, visit www.mta.info or phone 718-817-8700.

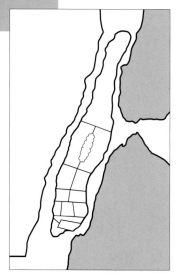

The Boroughs

Queens

When the British forced Dutch New York to surrender, they named Queens for Catherine of Braganza, England's first tea-drinking queen. Queens is nearly as big as Manhattan, Staten Island, and the Bronx combined. Home to Shea Stadium, the Aqueduct Race Track, and the National Tennis Center, which hosts the annual U.S. Open Tennis Championship, this sprawling borough is mostly residential. Immigrants from around the world have settled here, making Queens the most ethnically diverse county in the United States.

Accord Café
39-07 Prince St., corner Roosevelt Ave. (Jackson Heights)

This colorful, contemporary café serves a wide variety of tea drinks, sandwiches, noodle dishes, dumplings and other snacks – eight flavored tapioca pearl teas, a dozen fruity-green-tea blends, green tea frostees, and hot or cold "Hong Kong-style tea" with milk.

• Daily 11am-1am • Subway: Seven train to Flushing Main St. • Tel. 718-321-3820 • Cash only $

Aladdin Sweet Shop & Restaurant
37-14 73rd St. (Jackson Heights)

Enjoy sweet Indian snacks such as *burfi* pistachio sweets, *jallebi* fritters, *rasgullah* cream cheese balls, and *galub jamum* dumplings with a cup of chai.
• Daily 10am-1am • Subway: 7 train to 74th St.; E/F/G/R trains to Roosevelt Ave. • Tel. 718-424-6900 • Credit card minimum $20 • Cup of tea. Full menu. Snacks. Sweets. $

Delhi Palace Sweets
37-07 74th St. (Jackson Heights)

Indian sweets with chai or a full meal.
• Daily 11:30am-10:30pm • Subway: 7 train to 74th St., E/F/G/R trains to Roosevelt Ave. • Tel. 718-507-0666
• Major credit cards • Cup of tea. Full meals. Snacks. Sweets. $

Maharaja Quality Sweets Shop & Vegetarian Restaurant
73-10 37th Ave. (Jackson Heights)

Maharaja's confections are fit for a queen. Some of the delicious pink, green, orange or white morsels shimmer with edible silver and gold leaf decorations.
• Daily 10am-10pm • Subway: 7 train to 74th St.; E/F/G/R to 37th Rd. (Roosevelt Ave.) • Tel. 718-505-2680 • Major credit cards • Cup of tea. Full menu. Snacks. Sweets. $

Tai Pan Bakery
42-05B Main St. and 37-25 Main St. (Flushing)

A wide assortment of inexpensive, freshly-baked Chinese-style cakes, sweet breads, four types of egg-custard tarts, hot snacks and sweet or savory buns are sold here. Competitive bubble tea prices. Additional location in Chinatown (page 15).
• Daily 7:30am-8pm • Subway: Seven train to Flushing Main St. • Tel. 718-461-8668
• Cash only • www.taipan-bakery.com

Ten Ren
135-18 Roosevelt Ave. (Flushing)

Multiple locations. See flagship listing on page 16.
• Daily 10am-8pm • Subway: Seven train to Flushing Main St. • Tel. 718-461-9305
• Major credit cards • www.tenren.usa.com
• Hot tea. Bubble tea. $.

Serendipitea, a company devoted to premium grade, organic loose-leaf tea, founded ten years ago by Tomislav Podreka, is based in Long Island City.

The Voelker Orth Museum, Bird Sanctuary and Victorian Garden
149-19 38th Ave. at 149th St. (Flushing)

The Voelker Orth museum, located seven blocks from the subway station, is worth the hike. The petal-pink, Queen Anne Victorian house, surrounded by a bird sanctuary and lovely cottage garden, seems out-of-place among its drab, contemporary neighbors. But long ago, the area was populated with such elegant homes. This estate

was donated by Elisabeth Orth who lived in the house until her death in 1995. Following her wishes, the home and grounds have been completely restored into a living landmark to preserve the historical and cultural heritage of Queens and Long Island.

Tea fans gather in the parlor to review a presentation about the social history of tea before enjoying homemade sweets, savories and freshly brewed loose tea. In fair weather, tea may be served under a tent in the garden. Indoors or out, the menu, which changes seasonally, is based on historic recipes and includes two cucumber-watercress sandwiches and a crab-carrot salad. The scone recipe dates to 1867 and is served with two types of homemade lemon curd or jam. As this was a German household, Black Forest cake is a featured dessert along with fresh fruit, cookies and bonbons. After tea, guests are treated to a tour of the house and garden, which are available for weddings and private parties. The museum also hosts concerts, horticultural lectures, workshops, and walking tours.

• Wed., Sat.-Sun. 1-4pm • Subway: 7 train to Main St. or LIRR to Murray Hill Station • Tel. 718-359-6227 • Cash or check only • www.voelkerorthmuseum.org • Full afternoon set tea and program presented once a month. Reservations required. $$

To Tea Or Not To Tea

A refresher course on the various ways, brews, and times to enjoy a relaxing cuppa.

Afternoon Tea

Described on some menus as a *set tea* or *full tea*, afternoon tea is an elegant, light meal accompanied by a choice of freshly-brewed teas served by the pot. A pot of hot water should be provided to dilute strong tea or brew a second cup. Formally presented, all-at-once on a tiered server, or a la carte, courses consist of scones, several kinds of crustless finger sandwiches or other savories, followed by sweet treats such as petits fours, custard or cake, cookies, éclairs, etc. Traditionally served between three and five o'clock, some venues offer afternoon tea from lunch on. Hotels often offer a glass of champagne, sherry, or port, especially when teatime spills over into the cocktail hour.

Black Tea

Black tea is fully-oxidized. Freshly-plucked green leaves are withered and then twisted or rolled to release and oxidize natural enzymes. Finally, the leaves are dried to become the familiar black leaf noted for its rich, full-bodied brew.

Blended Teas

Teas from a variety of estates are often combined to ensure a quality product under changing agricultural conditions. Flowers, fruit, herbs, spices, and scented or flavored oils may be added. Earl Grey is an example of a blended tea.

Bocha

Bocha (BOW-chah) is broth-like, buttered, and salted Tibetan tea. Sometimes referred to as *po cha* or *bhoe cha*.

Bubble Tea

Also called boba, milk, pearl, sago or tapioca tea, bubble tea originated in Taiwan in the 1980s. The roots of the potato-like cassava plant are ground, mixed with brown sugar, and cooked. Starch from sago palm is sometimes used. Marble-sized "pearls" are added to hot or cold, green or black tea along with fruit, or fruit juice, and milk. The mix is shaken to produce bubbles and served with a fat straw to suck the chewy pearls.

Chai

Masala chai (*chai* rhymes with *tie*), or spiced tea, is a drink made with ground black tea infused with milk, sugar, and a variety of spices such as cardamom, cinnamon, cloves, ginger, or pepper. In India, it is traditionally drunk from a glass or disposable pottery cup. Americans drink chocolate chai, chai lattes, chai smoothies, green tea, and herbal chai beverages, including chai made with soy milk.

Cream Tea
Tea is sometimes taken with milk, but never cream. It's too rich. The term *cream tea* refers to a snack of scones served with Devon, double or clotted (cooked) cream, jam and a pot of tea. Sometimes called *light* tea, cream tea is served late morning to early evening and might include sandwiches or a piece of cake.

Dim Sum
Linked to the Chinese tradition of *yum cha*, or drinking tea, *dim sum* literally means to touch your heart. This Cantonese brunch, consisting of sweet and savory appetizers, to be enjoyed with tea, spread to Hong Kong and eventually the States.

Gong Fu
Gong Fu, also called *Kong Fu*, is the traditional way of tasting tea in the Fujian and Guangdong provinces of southeastern China. The ceremony highlights the spirit of tea, tea etiquette, skilled preparation, pouring, and evaluating tea's quality. Typically, the ceremony is performed for no more than four guests, using a tiny earthenware pot and miniature tea bowls or straight-sided cups. The leaves are infused several times - the first to rinse and heat the cups while "waking the leaves up," the second to enjoy the fragrance, the third for flavor.

Green Tea
Green tea is the brew's oldest form. The leaves are steamed, rolled, and dried, not oxidized. Chinese varieties tend to be more mellow than "grassy" Japanese teas.

High Tea
Frequently confused with afternoon tea, high tea is "dinner in all but name," according to Mrs. Beeton, the Victorian domestic diva. The name is said to refer to the fact that this meal was eaten at a high dining table rather than a low parlor table reserved for afternoon tea. The menu features savory fare such as fish and chips (fries), meat or fish pie, bangers (sausages) and mash (potatoes), baked beans on toast, cheese sandwiches, and simple desserts such as fruit pie or plain cake, washed down with strong, milky tea. Originally a working class supper served about six o'clock, high tea entrees are often available as early as noon, or as late as closing-time, in places that serve British pub grub.

Honeybush
Honeybush is an herbal infusion made with South Africa's *Cyclopia* plant. The slightly sweet drink has no caffeine and is delicious hot or cold. It is often used to flavor green, black or Rooibos teas.

Lemon Myrtle
Lemon myrtle is an herbal infusion brewed with Australia's *Backhousia citriodora* plant. The caffeine-free beverage is high in vitamin C and has a sweet, lemon-lime flavor and fragrance.

Merienda
In many Hispanic cultures, *merienda (merry-en-DA),* Spanish for snack, is known as "the fourth meal." Children eat it after school, workers for an afternoon break, but it might be eaten all day long. It is similar to afternoon tea, but more substantial.

Oolong Tea
This partially-oxidized tea traditionally comes from China and Formosa. The flavor of so-called "brown" tea is a "compromise" between black and green teas.

Puerh
A black or green tea that has been allowed to oxidize a second time. It improves with age and may be compressed into shapes or left loose.

Rooibos
South African *Rooibos (ROY-bus)* or "Red Bush tea" is a caffeine-free herbal infusion, high in Vitamin C and antioxidant properties. It is thought to relieve insomnia, headaches, nausea, asthma, and allergies.

Tisane
Tisanes (tih-ZAHN) are brewed with herbs, flowers, fruit, root, berries, bark, or the leaves of any plant other than *Camellia sinensis.* They do not contain caffeine.

White Tea
Young tea buds from are plucked before opening, withered to drive off moisture, then gently dried. The curled buds have a silvery-white color and brew a straw-colored liquid. Originally grown in the Fujian province of China, white teas are now also manufactured in Sri Lanka and Darjeeling.

Tea in the City: New York
An index to sipping and shopping

Alphabetical list of tea rooms

Shopping Sites for Tea Lovers